BITCOIN CONSOLIDATED

VOLUME 1

DAVID MARULLI

PROOF OF WORK PRESS

Bitcoin Consolidated: Volume 1

Published by PROOF OF WORK PRESS
Aurora, CO

www.bitcoinconsolidated.com

Bitcoin Block Height as of Publication: 926,169

ISBN: 979-8-9988041-0-6 (paperback)
ISBN: 979-8-9988041-2-0 (hardcover)
ISBN: 979-8-9988041-1-3 (ebook)

BUSINESS & ECONOMICS / Bitcoin & Cryptocurrencies

Cover design by Graphroots Design.
Interior design by Bryan Canter.
All copyright owned by David Marulli.

Figure 1 "Block Subsidy Table" by Wicked (@w_s_bitcoin)

CONTENTS

Bitcoin does not adapt to the world;
the world adapts to Bitcoin.

Introduction

The first time I heard about Bitcoin was around 2012. A friend of mine was announcing it from the rooftops. I distinctly remember two things: I thought he was annoying, and I thought Bitcoin was ridiculous. My immediate assumption was that it was like the tokens you'd get at Chuck E. Cheese—valuable only within a small but irrelevant circle. At best, Bitcoin seemed like an obscure hobby for nerdy enthusiasts, something bound to fade into obscurity.

Bitcoin continued drifting in and out of my awareness. By 2016, I had acknowledged it as something real, but I had no grasp of its significance. It still seemed just like another speculative asset, something people traded, lost money on, or bragged about when the price rose. Beyond that, it meant nothing to me.

You see, for thirty years, I've been a commercial real estate broker, income property analyst, and consultant. My career has been deeply embedded in capital markets, asset valuation, spreadsheets, contracts, and financial strategy. I've analyzed deals, structured investments, and navigated market cycles. That said, even though my profession gave me a solid understanding of money and value, I often felt trapped.

I had been drawn to trading equities for a long time, but real estate kept me too busy to truly explore it. I monitored market trends and occasionally dabbled in the stock market but never fully engaged until 2019, when I opened a TD Ameritrade account (originally a Scottrade account, now both part of Charles Schwab). I did some research, picked a few companies, and went back to work.

Then came March 2020. We all know what happened next.

My stocks crashed, and my entire pipeline of commercial real estate deals disintegrated. Banks warned us their economists predicted a potential 30%–40% decline in commercial property values (they were wrong).[1] Lenders refused to finance anything at current prices. The entire market froze.

A wave of anxiety swept over me as everything I'd built threatened to come to a screeching halt. Yet instead of shutting down, my mind latched onto something new: trading. I became hyperfocused on technical analysis, chart patterns, candlesticks, and indicators (discussed in Chapter 13). I devoured information while trading with real money—not the smartest approach at the start. I suffered losses and missed great opportunities. Over time, though, I improved. Mistakes stung less. Wins came more frequently. For the first time, I felt I was finally pursuing something I genuinely wanted.

That's when Bitcoin entered the picture.

At first, I traded Bitcoin mining stocks, still misunderstanding Bitcoin as risky, volatile and detached from reality. But something about it drew me in, commanding my attention. At some point in 2022, my mind magnetized to Bitcoin with an intensity I'd never experienced before. Soon after, I put everything else aside and became completely fixated. How could something so fundamentally important exist, and I barely understood it? This realization was the true hurdle. Bitcoin was dramatically different from anything familiar, making comprehension challenging. Yet grasping Bitcoin became the key to unlocking a new reality—a doorway to personal freedom, economic sovereignty, and monetary awakening.

From that moment onward, I would never be the same.

This state of mind has only intensified, unfolding in ways I never could have imagined. I am humbled by and forever grateful to Bitcoin.

Eventually, I challenged myself to list the ten most important insights I'd learned about Bitcoin. However, that list exploded into hundreds of discoveries. Bullet points became paragraphs, paragraphs grew into pages, pages evolved into chapters.

This book is the initial distillation of my extensive efforts researching, writing, recording, discussing, and obsessively refining everything I've come to know about Bitcoin.

Through it, I hope that you will learn, as I did, to see the world through a new lens—one where Bitcoin can help you reshape your relationship with money and with life.

CHAPTER 1

INCEPTION

BITCOIN CHANGED the course of human history, emerging from the turmoil of the worst economic crisis since the Great Depression, precisely when humanity needed it most. In October 2008, at the height of this upheaval, a groundbreaking document appeared online: *Bitcoin: A Peer-to-Peer Electronic Cash System.*[1] Published anonymously by the enigmatic figure known as Satoshi Nakamoto, this white paper outlined a monetary system independent of governments, banks, or intermediaries, secured entirely by mathematics and cryptography (the practice of encoding information to ensure secure communication).

Traditional currencies depend on centralized authorities that effortlessly create and manipulate money, but Bitcoin—often referred to by its ticker symbol BTC—introduced a fundamentally different approach. Instead of printing money at will, Bitcoin requires verifiable effort—known as Proof of Work (PoW)—where computational energy is expended to verify authenticity, integrity, and value. Rather than relying on trusted third parties, Bitcoin's security relies entirely on cryptographic proof and decentralized consensus, making it transparent, open-source, and free from centralized control. No single entity, government, or even its creator could control or corrupt it. More than simply another currency, Bitcoin represented encoded defiance of the established financial order.

Upon entering the scene, Bitcoin went largely unnoticed, dismissed by many as improbable. It was considered an obscure cryptographic curiosity that spread slowly among cryptographers, libertarians, and cypherpunks before reaching the wider community. Early adopters quickly recognized Bitcoin's revolutionary innovation: the separation of money from state control. Historically, governments monopolized money creation to influence economies, wage wars, and uphold power structures. Bitcoin offered an unprecedented alternative, governed solely by transparent, mathematical rules rather than human authority, a philosophical and societal shift that completely altered the relationship between citizens and their governments.

Since late 2009, Bitcoin's price has surged from approximately $0.00099 per coin to $118,000.00 in July of 2025,[2] an astonishing increase of over 11.9 billion percent. Yet Bitcoin's significance runs deeper than its price; it symbolizes a groundbreaking transformation. What began as an obscure monetary experiment evolved into a global force reshaping finance precisely at the historic moment when trust in traditional financial institutions was severely shaken.

Bitcoin's breakthrough design directly confronted the systemic failures exposed by the financial crisis. Fiat currencies rely entirely on trust in issuing governments, making them vulnerable to endless printing, manipulation, and value dilution.[3] Bitcoin, in stark contrast, has a mathematically unalterable fixed supply—exactly 21 million coins—rendering it immune from such manipulation (more on this in Chapter 4).

In May 2010, Bitcoin facilitated its first real-world transaction when 10,000 bitcoin[4] were exchanged for two pizzas in Florida. At the time, those coins were nearly worthless; today, they'd be valued at over a billion dollars. Despite constant skepticism, ridicule from economists, and repeated premature obituaries in the media, Bitcoin has thrived. Every challenge strengthened it, gradually transforming skepticism into curiosity, curiosity into belief, and belief into awe.

One of the most extraordinary aspects of Bitcoin's story isn't its price or disruptive power. It's the mystery surrounding its creator. After introducing the most revolutionary monetary system ever created, Satoshi Nakamoto simply disappeared. They never claimed credit, never spent their vast Bitcoin fortune, and never revealed their identity. Instead, in April 2011, Satoshi gently handed control to the community, stating they had "moved on to other things," and stepped away forever. Bitcoin needed no central figure to drive its development, and by disappearing, Satoshi demonstrated that the system could sustain itself without any single point of control. Yet the question remains: What did someone with such a remarkable intellect move onto after Bitcoin? Did Satoshi venture into deeper realms of technology, shift toward introspective spiritual or existential pursuits, or remain quietly observant, watching their creation change the world from afar? Perhaps they're no longer alive, their identity forever enshrined in mystery.

Like electricity, automobiles, or the internet, Bitcoin's true impact will become fully evident only in hindsight. Decades from now, people will look back at this era and wonder, "Imagine being alive when Bitcoin was affordable." But even given the chance today, most would hesitate to act. Recognizing a paradigm shift as it unfolds requires more than knowledge.

It requires vision.

And above all, it requires conviction.

CHAPTER 2

WHO IS SATOSHI NAKAMOTO?

BITCOIN EXISTS WITHOUT A LEADER. It has no headquarters, no CEO, and no government backing it. At the core of its creation lies a profound, seemingly impossible mystery: Satoshi Nakamoto.

Bitcoin shouldn't exist, not just because a decentralized, self-sustaining monetary network was long considered impossible, but because whoever created it should never have been able to vanish without a trace. How does someone conceive a new form of money capable of dismantling traditional financial power structures and then disappear completely, leaving no clues, no traces, nothing? Who possesses the intellectual brilliance required to uncover and engineer Bitcoin's elemental forces, the foresight to release it precisely when humanity needed it most, and the discipline to abandon it, refusing even a fraction of the immense potential wealth that it promised?

Such a person should not exist. And yet, somehow, they did.

Satoshi Nakamoto is more than a pseudonym; it's an unprecedented creative force. Satoshi was not merely a brilliant programmer and gifted cryptographer, they had profound insight into economics, cryptography, game theory, and human psychology.

They understood incentives, vulnerabilities, human behavior, and how systems of power operate. Satoshi carefully designed Bitcoin as an unstoppable system: trustless, decentralized, incorruptible, and immune from traditional forms of manipulation.

Satoshi's brilliance wasn't made evident just through the act of creating Bitcoin, but in deliberately removing themselves from it afterward. Through online forums, email correspondence, and the original BitcoinTalk message board, Satoshi patiently explained technical concepts to the early community, always reinforcing the vision of decentralization, trustlessness, and financial sovereignty. Satoshi's humility was as evident in these interactions as it was in the anonymous departure. By vanishing completely, Satoshi guaranteed that Bitcoin belonged to no individual, no government, and no corporation. It belonged to everyone and no one simultaneously.

There are theories that Satoshi was actually a team of people, but I think that's impossible. The probability that a group of individuals in 2008 had the collective genius, vision, and humility to create Bitcoin, maintain perfect anonymity, and resist the immense temptation of fame and fortune is too low to be credible. Human nature is too flawed and too susceptible to greed and pride—especially in groups, which would inevitably fracture under the weight of secrecy, threats of betrayal, and pressures of ego. Someone would have revealed something.

But one extraordinary individual with a uniquely brilliant, disciplined, almost otherworldly mind could indeed do all of this and then vanish without a trace. Satoshi's decision to step away from Bitcoin, leaving behind a fortune of over a million coins (today worth over 100 billion dollars) completely untouched, is perhaps the single greatest demonstration of restraint in the record of civilization.

When I reflect on Satoshi, I think of Leonardo da Vinci, whose genius transcended human limitations through bridging art, science, and philosophy. Da Vinci described art and invention as the pursuit of revealing the hidden truths embedded within nature itself. His profound mastery was astonishing, manifesting in drawings and designs so precise and visionary, it was as if they glimpsed the future and brought back blueprints from another age.

Satoshi's creation feels exactly like that. Every element of Bitcoin is perfectly aligned and meticulously balanced. Despite the incredible engineering of Bitcoin, it feels as though it was waiting to be discovered, a perfect monetary system hidden within mathematics itself, requiring only someone with enough clarity, intelligence, and vision to reveal it.

Yet unlike Leonardo da Vinci, who left behind a face to accompany his legacy, Satoshi disappeared without one. They claimed no recognition, sought no personal glory, desired no riches nor fame. They simply released Bitcoin into the world and stepped quietly into the shadows, never to return.

Satoshi once wrote: "If you don't believe me or don't get it, I don't have time to try to convince you, sorry."[1]

These words aren't dismissive; they're certain. Satoshi knew most people wouldn't immediately grasp Bitcoin's significance. They understood that arguing or convincing skeptics was futile. Bitcoin was built to prove itself over time, and it has.

Today, Bitcoin is the hardest form of money humanity has ever known, reshaping global finance and proving the viability of a stateless, incorruptible monetary system. And at its very heart stands Satoshi Nakamoto—a name without a face. A mind that changed the world yet left no trace. Perhaps that was precisely the point. Bitcoin was never about Satoshi—it was always about us.

The future belongs to those who understand it.

CHAPTER 3

THE GENESIS BLOCK

SIXTEEN YEARS AGO, Bitcoin entered our world through a singular event: the creation of the "genesis block."

A blockchain is essentially a digital ledger, a chain of connected blocks, each containing records of transactions. Bitcoin created the first blockchain, and it is unlike any other. It began with a foundational block known as the genesis block, mined on January 3, 2009, by Satoshi Nakamoto.

Mining refers to the competitive process of using computational energy to solve mathematical puzzles, called hashing, which allows new blocks of transaction data to be securely attached to the previous blocks in the chain. On average, each block (bundle of transactions) holds between 2,000 and 4,000 individual transactions. Miners are entities operating specialized computers or groups of computers designed explicitly for Bitcoin mining. Miners who successfully solve these puzzles get to attach the current block of transactions to the previous block and receive a reward known as the "block subsidy," initially set at 50 BTC per mined block (block rewards/halvings will be discussed in Chapter 4).

Known technically as "Block 0," the genesis block is unique.

Unlike every block that followed, it has no predecessor, contains no transactional history, and references no previous hash. It wasn't mined competitively; rather, Satoshi hard coded this block directly into Bitcoin's software as a symbolic act, marking the official beginning of a monetary revolution. Due to the way Satoshi coded Bitcoin, the first block reward of 50 BTC is permanently unspendable, locked forever in the blockchain's foundational block. This might seem like an oversight, but it was deliberate, reinforcing Bitcoin's purity of inception: no immediate personal benefit for its creator, no hidden advantage, and transparency from day one. This act was free from self-interest and set a powerful precedent of integrity and trust right from the start.

Embedded within this initial block was a subtle yet powerful message quoted from a newspaper printed on the same day:

"The Times 03/Jan/2009 Chancellor on brink of second bailout for banks."[1]

On the surface, this served as a timestamp, to show that Bitcoin hadn't been secretly created earlier. But on a deeper level, it was a clear indictment of the traditional financial system. Satoshi referenced the ongoing global financial crisis, highlighting how banks had recklessly risked financial stability and were subsequently bailed out by governments at public expense. Bitcoin's creation wasn't just technological innovation, it was a pointed critique, an antivirus, intentionally launched at a moment when trust in traditional finance was collapsing.

At that time, Bitcoin had no market value, and no transactions immediately followed the creation of the genesis block. But the foundation had been laid. Soon after, miners began competing, using Proof of Work (PoW), a method demanding real-world energy, to secure each new block and add value to each block subsidy. Every newly mined block linked irreversibly to the previous one, forming an unbreakable, incorruptible historical ledger: a blockchain. This immutable chain became Bitcoin's proof-of-integrity, a permanent and reliable record upon which trustless financial transactions could be built.

Thus, the genesis block was not merely Bitcoin's technical starting point. It was a declaration of independence, the first breath of a financial system destined to transform our world.

CHAPTER 4

THE HALVING

UNDERSTANDING BITCOIN'S halving transforms how you think about money. It reveals the true depth of the precision and planning behind Bitcoin's scarcity, an aspect of value not usually considered by traditional finance. The Halving isn't solely a technical event. Every halving represents a seismic shift embedded within Bitcoin's DNA, automatically reshaping incentives, miner behavior, and global perceptions of value.

Every 210,000 blocks, approximately every four years (known as epochs), Bitcoin undergoes this critical event. With flawless mathematical precision, the number of new bitcoin entering circulation is cut in half (see Figure 1). No central authority dictates this change; no government announces it. The Halving simply occurs, like clockwork—built into Bitcoin's very existence.

When Satoshi Nakamoto engineered Bitcoin (BTC), they designed it to follow a predictable issuance schedule hard coded into its protocol:

- 2009–2012: 50 BTC per block (10,500,000 BTC mined)
- 2012–2016: 25 BTC per block (5,250,000 BTC mined)
- 2016–2020: 12.5 BTC per block (2,625,000 BTC mined)
- 2020–2024: 6.25 BTC per block (1,312,500 BTC mined)
- 2024–2028: 3.125 BTC per block (656,250 BTC mined)

Block Height	Halving	Block Subsidy			Mined Supply (BTC)	Mined Supply (%)	Date
		Binary (sats)	Decimal (sats)	Decimal (BTC)			
0	0	100101010000001011111001001000000000	5,000,000,000	50.00000000	0	0.00000000	Jan 3, 2009
210,000	1	10010101000000101111110010010000000	2,500,000,000	25.00000000	10,500,000.00000000	50.00000006	Nov 28, 2012
420,000	2	1001010100000010111111001001000000	1,250,000,000	12.50000000	15,750,000.00000000	75.00000008	Jul 9, 2016
630,000	3	100101010000001011111100100100000	625,000,000	6.25000000	18,375,000.00000000	87.50000010	May 11, 2020
840,000	4	10010101000000101111110010010000	312,500,000	3.12500000	19,687,500.00000000	93.75000010	Apr 20, 2024
1,050,000	5	1001010100000010111111001001000	156,250,000	1.56250000	20,343,750.00000000	96.87500011	2028
1,260,000	6	100101010000001011111100101000	78,125,000	0.78125000	20,671,875.00000000	98.43750011	2032
1,470,000	7	10010101000000101111110011100	39,062,500	0.39062500	20,835,937.50000000	99.21875011	2036
1,680,000	8	1001010100000010111111001110	19,531,250	0.19531250	20,917,968.75000000	99.60937511	2040
1,890,000	9	100101010000001011111100111001	9,765,625	0.09765625	20,958,984.37500000	99.80468761	2044
2,100,000	10	10010101000000101111110011100	4,882,812	0.04882812	20,979,492.18750000	99.90234386	2048
2,310,000	11	1001010100000010111111001011111	2,441,406	0.02441406	20,989,746.09270000	99.95117198	2052
2,520,000	12	100101010000001011111101111	1,220,703	0.01220703	20,994,873.04530000	99.97558604	2056
2,730,000	13	10010101000000101111101111	610,351	0.00610351	20,997,436.52160000	99.98779307	2060
2,940,000	14	1001010100000010100000111	305,175	0.00305175	20,998,718.25870000	99.99389658	2064
3,150,000	15	100101010000001010000011	152,587	0.00152587	20,999,359.12620000	99.99694833	2068
3,360,000	16	10010101000000010000101	76,293	0.00076293	20,999,679.55890000	99.99847420	2072
3,570,000	17	100101010000000010	38,146	0.00038146	20,999,839.77420000	99.99923713	2076
3,780,000	18	10010101010000001	19,073	0.00019073	20,999,919.88080000	99.99961859	2080
3,990,000	19	1001010101000000	9,536	0.00009536	20,999,959.93410000	99.99980993	2084
4,200,000	20	100101010100000	4,768	0.00004768	20,999,979.95970000	99.99990468	2088
4,410,000	21	10010101010000	2,384	0.00002384	20,999,989.97250000	99.99995236	2092
4,620,000	22	1001010101000	1,192	0.00001192	20,999,994.97890000	99.99997610	2096
4,830,000	23	100101010100	596	0.00000596	20,999,997.48210000	99.99998812	2100
5,040,000	24	100101010	298	0.00000298	20,999,998.73370000	99.99999408	2104
5,250,000	25	10010101	149	0.00000149	20,999,999.35960000	99.99999706	2108
5,460,000	26	1001010	74	0.00000074	20,999,999.67240000	99.99999855	2112
5,670,000	27	1001010	37	0.00000037	20,999,999.82780000	99.99999929	2116
5,880,000	28	10010	18	0.00000018	20,999,999.90550000	99.99999966	2120
6,090,000	29	1001	9	0.00000009	20,999,999.94300000	99.99999983	2124
6,300,000	30	100	4	0.00000004	20,999,999.96220000	99.99999993	2128
6,510,000	31	10	2	0.00000002	20,999,999.97060000	99.99999997	2132
6,720,000	32	1	1	0.00000001	20,999,999.97480000	99.99999999	2136
6,930,000	33		0	0.00000000	20,999,999.97690000	100.00000000	2140

Figure 1: Bitcoin Block Subsidy Table

This halving schedule guarantees Bitcoin's scarcity over time, dramatically restricting the proliferation of new coins every four years. We're currently only in the fourth of thirty-two total halvings. By 2140, the last fraction of Bitcoin will be mined, reaching the ultimate supply cap of 21 million coins. At that point, Bitcoin will become fully issued, an event unprecedented in the history of money.

BITCOIN'S DIFFICULTY ADJUSTMENT: TIME BENT TO THE PROTOCOL

Bitcoin's consistent issuance schedule is strictly maintained by the Difficulty Adjustment mechanism. Approximately every two weeks, after every 2,016 blocks, the network recalibrates its mining difficulty to maintain a stable ten-minute interval between new blocks. If miners collectively increase computational power and blocks begin forming too quickly, the algorithm automatically makes mining more challenging. Conversely, if mining activity slows down and blocks form too slowly, it becomes easier. This elegant, automatic recalibration ensures Bitcoin's issuance remains precisely on schedule, independent of external circumstances, like market volatility or human interference. Bitcoin does not adapt to the world; the world adapts to Bitcoin.

ACCELERATING SCARCITY

Each halving intensifies Bitcoin's scarcity, pushing ownership of a whole coin increasingly out of reach. Further constricting supply:

- As of early 2025, approximately 2.3 to 3.7 million bitcoin are estimated to be permanently lost (more on this in Chapter 10).[1]

- Institutional investors, corporations, and sovereign wealth funds are accumulating bitcoin, removing vast quantities from circulation indefinitely.
- Long-term holders, recognizing Bitcoin's true value, rarely part with their holdings. According to Bitwise Asset Management with data from River Financial and BitMEX, as of December 31, 2024, 69.4% of the available Bitcoin supply is owned by individuals and only 1.4% by governments.[2] (See Figure 2.) These stats will change as institutions, businesses, and governments buy more bitcoin, but those who know what it is aren't selling to them.

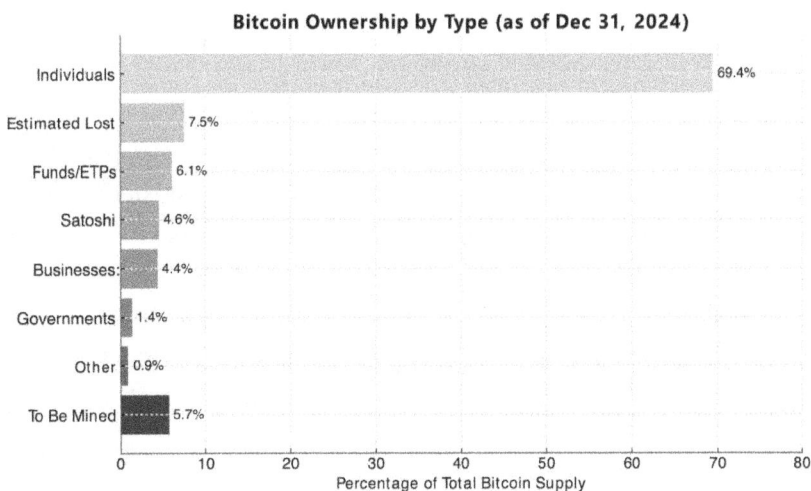

Bitcoin Ownership by Type (as of Dec 31, 2024)

Individuals	69.4%
Estimated Lost	7.5%
Funds/ETPs	6.1%
Satoshi	4.6%
Businesses	4.4%
Governments	1.4%
Other	0.9%
To Be Mined	5.7%

Percentage of Total Bitcoin Supply

Figure 2: Bitcoin Ownership by Type as of December 31, 2024

As supply shrinks and demand expands, Bitcoin's accessibility diminishes rapidly. By 2032, acquiring a whole bitcoin might be impossible for the vast majority of people. By 2044, simply owning 0.1 BTC will represent significant wealth (discussed further in Chapter 15).

Yet, Bitcoin remains functional at every scale. Each bitcoin can be denominated into 100 million smaller units called satoshis, or "sats" for short, much like how a dollar can be divided into 100 cents. These units are perfectly fungible, as each satoshi is interchangeable with any other, so just as you don't need to spend an entire dollar for small purchases, you don't need to use a full bitcoin for everyday transactions. This extreme divisibility ensures bitcoin remains practical and accessible as a global currency, even as its scarcity intensifies (discussed further in Chapter 18).

MINERS AND THE LONG-TERM SECURITY MODEL

Each halving also reshapes Bitcoin's security model. Currently, miners primarily earn through newly minted coins: the block subsidy. While the number of bitcoin rewarded per block decreases with each halving, the actual economic value of the subsidy continues to rise significantly due to Bitcoin's price appreciation driven by increasing adoption and scarcity. Over the next 115 years, as the block subsidy approaches its eventual end, miners' incentives will gradually shift to rely more heavily on transaction fees. These fees, rather than increasing in cost per transaction, will become plentiful due to growing network use. By the time the final halving occurs, transaction fees alone will serve to support miners, similar to how toll roads maintain operations through widespread and consistent use, rather than increasing the toll price per vehicle.

Because of this, Bitcoin's miners, incentivized by both scarcity and fees, continue to secure and strengthen the network through their combined computational output. This ensures Bitcoin's decentralization and robustness, independent of centralized financial authority or political influence.

As a new monetary phenomenon, the halving represents a paradigm shift in monetary thinking. It introduces:

- True scarcity, guaranteed by mathematics rather than trust in human institutions (see Figure 3).
- Predictable issuance, unlike the inflation[3] cycles driven by unpredictable fiat currencies.
- A decreasing rather than expanding supply, defying historical monetary patterns.

And so, each halving is a wake-up call. It's a powerful reminder of Bitcoin's fundamental principles, encouraging holders to tighten their grip and skeptics to reconsider their stance. The Halving is not just economical, it's philosophical. It embodies Bitcoin's defiance of traditional monetary systems, reshaping human understanding of value itself.

BITCOIN'S
MONETARY POLICY

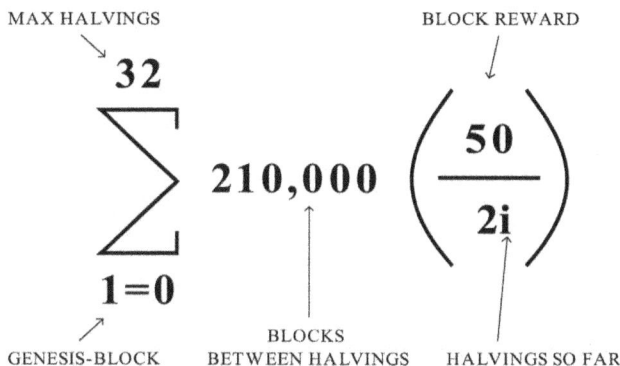

$$\text{MAX HALVINGS} \qquad \text{BLOCK REWARD}$$

$$\sum_{1=0}^{32} 210{,}000 \left(\frac{50}{2^i} \right)$$

GENESIS-BLOCK · BLOCKS BETWEEN HALVINGS · HALVINGS SO FAR

Figure 3: Bitcoin's Monetary Policy Formula

Will you recognize the importance of securing your piece before its existing scarcity becomes impossible to ignore?

In the end, the Halving isn't just about fewer bitcoin being created, it's about how each halving compresses the opportunity to own a larger share before the world fully comprehends what's unfolding.

CHAPTER 5

ABSOLUTE MATHEMATICAL SCARCITY

BITCOIN HAS INTRODUCED humanity to a new form of economic intelligence as if it were something sent from the future to teach us a better way forward.

For centuries, humanity has searched for the perfect form of money, an asset capable of storing and transferring value reliably through time. Gold served this purpose for millennia but remained imperfect. Its supply was limited but continually expanded through mining, preventing it from ever becoming perfectly scarce. Fiat currencies, meanwhile, were manipulated and inflated by governments, subjecting entire populations to economic instability and wealth erosion.

Then came Bitcoin.

Bitcoin is the first and only asset governed by absolute mathematical scarcity. Its supply is permanently fixed and finite, enforced by mathematics, and invulnerable to manipulation or alteration.

This is the breakthrough.

Bitcoin's fixed supply is a revolution in economic philosophy. It challenges the very foundation of how humans interact with value.

Originally, referring to Bitcoin as "digital gold" was a helpful analogy for new learners due to gold's familiar quality of scarcity. However, this comparison no longer feels accurate or sufficient. Gold's scarcity, as opposed to Bitcoin's, isn't absolute. Beyond scarcity, Bitcoin significantly surpasses gold in portability, divisibility, and transferability. While gold is heavy, dense, visible, and difficult to move or subdivide practically, Bitcoin is weightless, invisible, instantly transferable, and infinitely divisible. Bitcoin transcends gold at every level, and ultimately, there's nothing truly comparable to Bitcoin—it is uniquely its own phenomenon.

Bitcoin operates on a monetary system where the supply schedule is known to the decimal point and was set in stone from the moment of inception. Bitcoin represents the ultimate store of value:

- Gold is scarce—but we keep finding more.
- Land is scarce—but we keep building higher.
- Bitcoin is absolutely scarce—no force in the universe can create more.

Unlike fiat, which loses purchasing power over time, Bitcoin absorbs economic energy and preserves it across generations. It separates money from the state in a way never before possible, eliminating the ability of governments and central banks to manipulate its supply for their own interests.

In a world where every fiat currency has eventually collapsed under the weight of inflation, Bitcoin operates in reverse—it becomes scarcer over time, meaning its purchasing power can only increase in the long term.

Understanding Bitcoin's absolute mathematical scarcity illuminates one of the unique features that makes Bitcoin resilient and superior to anything we have encountered before. Yet scarcity alone isn't sufficient; there must also be a secure, transparent method to enforce and manage it. How exactly does Bitcoin maintain its scarcity, verify ownership, and ensure that coins aren't duplicated, double-spent, or counterfeited? The answer lies within the interconnected framework of Bitcoin's network and the rules embedded in its foundational protocol.

CHAPTER 6

THE BASE LAYER – THE PROTOCOL, THE NETWORK, THE TIMECHAIN, AND THE ASSET

To GRASP the deeper meaning of Bitcoin, it is important to know that the innovative payment network isn't simply digital money. Bitcoin's base layer is a self-sustaining system made of four inseparable components: the Protocol, the Network, the Timechain (the Blockchain), and the Asset. Together, they form an autonomous, decentralized financial organism operating above manipulation or control.

THE PROTOCOL

The protocol is Bitcoin's rule book. It's the software code that defines how the network operates, how transactions are verified, and how new bitcoin come into existence. If Bitcoin is a self-sustaining organism, the protocol is its DNA.

The rules are enforced globally by thousands of independent nodes. Transactions must be valid and must not be double-spent. Blocks target roughly a ten-minute cadence, and issuance of new bitcoin into circulation follows a known schedule. Two mechanisms define this predictability. First is Proof of Work (PoW) mining, which requires tangible computational effort to propose new blocks, preventing arbitrary issuance. Second is the Difficulty Adjustment. Every 2,016 blocks—about every two weeks—the network automatically recalibrates mining difficulty to keep that ten-minute rhythm. If hash power rises, difficulty rises; if it falls, difficulty eases. Time bends to the protocol, not the other way around.

THE NETWORK

From those rules, a network forms. If we think of Bitcoin, the protocol, as the DNA, then the network is the circulatory system. It's a global, decentralized infrastructure composed of thousands of independent nodes and miners spread across the planet that communicate with one another, validate transactions, broadcast blocks, and maintain consensus on the state of the ledger.

Nodes are primarily software. Anyone with a capable computer and a reliable connection can run Bitcoin Core (Bitcoin network's software infrastructure), maintain a copy of the ledger, and verify everything independently. In practice, many people choose dedicated hardware to simplify setup and isolate resources. I run my node on an Umbrel at home for exactly that reason: It securely stores the chain data and keeps verification sovereign without touching my personal computer.

Roles interlock inside this decentralized organism:

- Full nodes independently verify transactions, enforce the protocol, and preserve the network's integrity. Transactions propagate to nodes first; miners only build on what the nodes accept.
- Miners provide the computational muscle, competing via PoW to assemble valid transactions into blocks and extend the ledger.

- Wallets are the user interface to keys. They don't "hold" coins so much as authorize movement. Custodial convenience exists, but this book explores why sovereign keys matter (see Chapter 10).

Every transaction undergoes the same consensus-based collaborative process—validation by nodes, inclusion by miners, and broadcasts to the network—delivering transparency, security, and practical finality.

THE TIMECHAIN

Satoshi Nakamoto didn't usually call it a "blockchain"; instead they often referenced it as a "timechain"—a subtle but essential distinction. Each block doesn't just store transactions; it seals them beneath a layer of work that's costly to redo. Each new block references the last, creating an irreversible chain through time.

Conceptually, the timechain can be compared to what ancient spiritual traditions call the Akashic Records—an all-encompassing archive. The difference is that Bitcoin's record is real, transparent, verifiable, and permanent. Altering a single block would require redoing the PoW for every subsequent block, an impossibility given the network's extraordinary hash power. The timechain is memory made public, auditable, and designed to outlast all of us.

THE ASSET

Out of this machinery comes the thing people actually hold: bitcoin (the unit). It is natively digital, easy to move, and trivial to verify. It subdivides into satoshis, making even small amounts obtainable and usable. Its supply is fixed by the rules mentioned previously; scarcity here isn't a slogan, it's a property the protocol defines, the network enforces, and the timechain anchors.

Practically, bitcoin serves as:

- A medium of exchange—value transferred without intermediaries over neutral rails.
- A store of value—digital property resistant to debasement and centralized discretion.
- An emerging settlement instrument—finalizing without a central counterparty.

THE HIERARCHY

If you start with the asset, it can look like numbers in a database. If you start with the rules, the peers who enforce them, and the record that compounds cost into the past, you see why that asset exists— and why it's different. Bitcoin's internal order runs from foundation to surface:

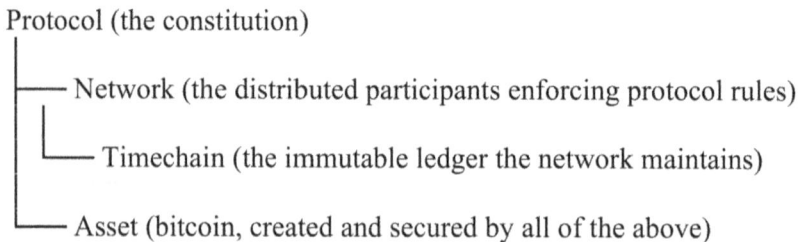

Protocol (the constitution)
- Network (the distributed participants enforcing protocol rules)
- Timechain (the immutable ledger the network maintains)
- Asset (bitcoin, created and secured by all of the above)

In short:

- Protocol = rules, algorithms, monetary policy, cryptography, difficulty, consensus mechanisms.
- Network = nodes, miners, hardware and software that run and enforce the rules.

- Timechain = permanent, public ledger resulting from the network, enforcing the rules.
- Asset = bitcoin, the monetary unit produced and secured by this integrated system.

Bitcoin is antifragile; it strengthens under pressure and adapts around chokepoints. If governments attempt censorship or interference, Bitcoin reroutes, rebalances, and continues forward. Together, the protocol, the network, the timechain, and the asset function as a unified base layer of a financial organism. Independent of its creator, it evolves and endures.

CHAPTER 7

THE SYSTEM – PROOF OF WORK, MINERS, AND HASH RATE

PROOF OF WORK: BITCOIN'S METABOLIC ENGINE

WHEN I WAS YOUNG, I recall television commercials for Smith Barney, whose slogan was, "We make money the old-fashioned way, we earn it." That phrase resonates deeply now that I've learned the concept of Bitcoin's Proof of Work (PoW). Fiat money isn't earned; it's conjured effortlessly into existence, and there's no real value in that. Bitcoin stands as fiat's antithesis, demanding verifiable proof: proof of energy expended, proof of real-world effort, proof that every bitcoin is genuinely earned.

Bitcoin's PoW is fundamental to its security, an incorruptible process converting electricity into economic value. Miners, operating specialized hardware known as ASIC miners (Application-Specific Integrated Circuits), compete to solve cryptographic puzzles. They deploy massive computational resources to discover a unique number called a nonce, which, when combined with transaction data and processed through the SHA-256 algorithm, yields a specific result known as a hash. For a block to be accepted, the hash must fall below the network's current difficulty target, which is

expressed by the number of leading zeros required in the hash. The
more zeros, the harder it is to find a valid nonce, and the more work
is required. Collectively, ASIC miners execute sextillions of these
calculations per second, generating significant heat as a byproduct.
Successfully finding a valid nonce grants the miner the right to add
a new block of verified transactions to Bitcoin's blockchain,
rewarding them with newly minted bitcoin—known as the block
subsidy or block reward—plus transaction fees. These fees are
small amounts paid by users to have their transactions confirmed,
usually just a few cents when the network is quiet (at the time of
writing, about $0.19), but rising during periods of congestion as
users compete for limited block space.

MINERS: GUARDIANS AND HEARTBEAT OF THE NETWORK

Miners range from individuals operating single ASIC machines at
home to massive industrial-scale data centers run by publicly traded
companies. Collectively, they secure the network, maintaining
decentralization and resilience by continuously validating transactions and competing to secure new blocks.

Critics frequently label Bitcoin's energy usage as wasteful, yet
many miners are active leaders in environmental stewardship,
driven to seek out the most affordable energy sources available.
Miners regularly harness stranded or intermittent energy sources,
transforming potentially wasted energy into economic and environmental benefits. A prominent example is methane capture: Methane,
a greenhouse gas with a global warming potential more than eighty
times greater than carbon dioxide over a twenty-year period,[1] regularly leaks from abandoned oil fields and landfills. Bitcoin miners
capture and combust this methane, converting it into significantly
less harmful carbon dioxide. Some miners even operate carbon-
negative facilities through methane-capture processes, actively

benefiting the environment by removing more greenhouse gases from the atmosphere than their operations produce.

Beyond methane capture, Bitcoin mining is becoming a catalyst for renewable energy adoption. Miners increasingly deploy renewable energy sources, such as solar, wind, and hydropower. In remote or underserved locations, miners establish initial energy grids that attract larger energy companies and investment, eventually facilitating comprehensive and stable energy infrastructure. In this way, mining accelerates renewable energy deployment, enhances regional economic stability, and improves local communities' access to reliable power.

Bitcoin mining hardware generates considerable heat. Rather than wasting this energy, miners now integrate mining infrastructure into buildings and community spaces. This heat can warm homes, swimming pools, greenhouses, and even support local agriculture. These innovations transform mining operations into valuable, integrated components of modern infrastructure, turning Bitcoin miners into digital or cryptographic trees that simultaneously secure the network and contribute directly to ecological sustainability.

Furthermore, Bitcoin miners play an essential role in stabilizing power grids by dynamically adjusting their energy consumption according to real-time grid conditions. During periods of excess energy production, miners absorb surplus electricity, thereby preventing waste. Conversely, during peak demand, miners rapidly reduce their power usage, redirecting energy back to essential services. The Electric Reliability Council of Texas (ERCOT) clearly illustrates this symbiotic relationship, effectively leveraging Bitcoin miners to balance grid loads, ensuring greater stability and efficiency.

In short, Bitcoin miners are not only securing a decentralized monetary system—they are actively contributing to a more sustainable and resilient global energy future.

THE HASH RATE: BITCOIN'S FORCE FIELD

The hash rate represents the cumulative computational power miners dedicate to securing the Bitcoin network. It is measured in hashes per second, progressing through terahashes (TH/s), peta-hashes (PH/s), exahashes (EH/s), and now zettahashes (ZH/s). One zettahash per second equals one sextillion (10^{21}) calculations every second, illustrating the immense computational force securing Bitcoin. For perspective, Bitcoin's hash rate far exceeds the computational power of the world's most powerful supercomputers combined, making it the strongest and most secure computer network ever assembled.

Bitcoin's hash rate has grown exponentially, evolving from a single computer in 2009 to surpassing one ZH/s today. This incredible computing force ensures network immutability; altering past transactions would require controlling more computational power than all miners worldwide combined—an economic and logistic impossibility.

The hash rate's strategic and geopolitical significance transcends technical security. Fred Thiel, CEO of Marathon Digital, argues that hash rate should be considered a national strategic asset, analogous to strategic petroleum reserves. Nations lacking significant domestic hash rate risk economic and geopolitical vulnerabilities. It's a realistic consideration that future geopolitical conflicts may revolve around computational dominance, specifically hash rate (discussed further in Chapter 25).

BITCOIN AS A SYSTEM

Together, PoW, miners, and hash rate form a robust, adaptive ecosystem. Bitcoin continually evolves, resiliently resisting geopolitical interference through decentralization. Miners freely migrate to regions offering stable and abundant energy sources, ensuring

Bitcoin's continuous operation and robustness against external threats. For example, HIVE Digital Technologies recently signed an agreement to develop a 100 MW hydroelectric-powered mining operation in Paraguay, tapping Itaipu Dam's renewable energy to add several exahashes per second to its global capacity.[2]

Beyond computational power, the hash rate is Bitcoin's immune system, safeguarding network integrity and ensuring Bitcoin's unstoppable trajectory. PoW is Bitcoin's metabolic engine, converting real-world energy into lasting economic value.

In a world of uncertainty, Bitcoin represents stability—secured one block at a time, powered by PoW, driven by miners, and protected by an ever-expanding, unparalleled computational force. Each block embodies real-world energy, permanently captured and secured within the block subsidy (the bitcoin brought into circulation), merging tangible effort with perfect scarcity to create enduring appreciation. When you own Bitcoin, no matter if it's many coins or just a fraction of one, you become synergized with this power. But how does Bitcoin enforce and verify ownership of this stored economic value? How does it practically ensure coins cannot be duplicated, double-spent, or counterfeited? The answer lies in Bitcoin's unique accounting method known as the Unspent Transaction Output model, or UTXO.

CHAPTER 8

UTXOs – The Inputs and Outputs of Bitcoin

ONE OF THE great revelations in understanding Bitcoin comes from grasping how it tracks ownership—not through traditional account balances but through an innovative accounting method known as Unspent Transaction Outputs (UTXOs). This revolutionary approach effectively solves the double-spending problem, a foundational breakthrough previously thought impossible.

Bitcoin does not operate like a traditional bank account. There are no ledger balances assigned to individuals, no centralized authority tracking ownership. Instead, Bitcoin's ledger is constructed from verifiable and distributed units of ownership known as UTXOs.

Imagine paying for something with a $100 bill. You don't retain the original bill after payment; instead, you receive smaller denominations as change. Similarly, if you have a UTXO of 1 BTC and send 0.4 BTC, the original UTXO is completely consumed. The transaction creates two new UTXOs: 0.4 BTC sent to the recipient, and 0.6 BTC returned to your wallet as change. This process is continuous as each transaction generates new UTXOs.

Consider an MP3 file or a PDF document. When you send one

of these digital files, you still keep your own copy, meaning digital files can be duplicated endlessly without restriction. For currency transfers, such duplication would be catastrophic because the same unit could be spent repeatedly (the "double-spending problem"). Bitcoin solves this by using a decentralized ledger (the blockchain), where every transaction is publicly recorded, verified by tens of thousands of nodes across the planet, and permanently locked in the world's most powerful computer network, making duplication or double-spending virtually impossible. Once Bitcoin is sent, it can't be resent or duplicated; it's permanently transferred. This elegant solution is foundational to Bitcoin's security and trust.

Bitcoin moves through this cycle of inputs and outputs because it must. It is a system built on constant movement and transformation. Each UTXO has its own history, tracing back through a chain of previous transactions all the way to its origination from mining rewards. This lineage is unchangeable and publicly verifiable, ensuring every bitcoin can be independently audited by anyone, at any time.

The structure of UTXOs is brilliant. Bitcoin is a model of continual economic dialogue between inputs and outputs. Just as a conversation progresses from one idea to the next, building upon what came before, Bitcoin's transactions represent an ongoing narrative of economic activity. Each transaction is an input that leads to new outputs, perpetually pushing the network forward.

On a deeper conceptual level, the UTXO model can be envisioned as neural pathways within the brain. Every neural pathway is unique, transmitting signals and generating distinct responses, evolving continuously based on experience and new stimuli. Similarly, UTXOs represent unique transactional pathways, each interaction creating new pathways and possibilities, securing and preserving the integrity and fluidity of the Bitcoin ecosystem.

UTXO knowledge can fundamentally change your perception of value and time itself. Just as the discovery of zero transformed mathematics by introducing the concept of nothingness, enabling previously unimaginable divisibility, measurement, and precision, Bitcoin transforms money by introducing absolute verifiability. With Bitcoin's UTXO model, value becomes precisely traceable, divisible, and verifiable down to its smallest fraction. There is no ambiguity, no hidden manipulation, no fractional reserves—only pure, verifiable truth, secured and transparently expressed in cryptographic form.

This process mirrors fundamental laws of energy conservation, thermodynamics, and transformation. Energy cannot be created nor destroyed, only transferred. Similarly, Bitcoin transactions never duplicate or vanish; they evolve. A UTXO consumed becomes new UTXOs created, continuously cycling and preserving the system's integrity.

This concept extends further than Bitcoin itself, reflecting how effective organization and consolidation can streamline complexity in life. In Bitcoin ownership, maintaining and consolidating UTXOs is an essential form of maintenance. Over time, multiple small UTXOs can accumulate, leading to inefficiencies and higher transaction fees. Consolidating UTXOs involves merging these fragmented, smaller amounts into fewer, larger UTXOs, thus optimizing future transactions. Unlike traditional assets, such as real estate, which require ongoing management, from vacancies to repairs, Bitcoin management involves simpler but critical tasks: consolidating UTXOs, securing self-custody (protecting private keys/seed phrases), and continuously educating oneself about Bitcoin.

In addition to technical knowledge, understanding UTXO offers an insight into a profound shift in how humanity can track, store, and perceive value. Bitcoin did not just solve the double-spending problem; it reshaped our understanding of digital value itself, establishing a standard that will redefine money forever.

CHAPTER 9

WHERE AND HOW TO BUY BITCOIN

WHEN I first decided to buy Bitcoin, I was both excited and nervous. I knew I wanted to own Bitcoin, but I wasn't entirely sure how to do it. Like many newcomers, I had numerous questions and a lingering fear of making mistakes. Through careful research and some initial trial and error, I navigated the learning curve. I'm sharing these lessons so that you can confidently buy bitcoin without repeating my missteps.

CRYPTOCURRENCY EXCHANGES: CONNECTING TO THE BITCOIN NETWORK

Cryptocurrency exchanges are digital marketplaces that allow you to purchase bitcoin using traditional fiat currencies, like dollars or euros. Popular exchanges include Coinbase, Kraken, Gemini, Binance, and Bitfinex.

Signing up for an exchange typically involves providing personal information as part a process called Know Your Customer (KYC). While this raises concerns around privacy, reputable exchanges use these procedures to comply with regulations and protect users from fraud and theft.

My initial experience involved Coinbase, which was straightforward to set up and use. After linking my checking account, I transferred fiat currency but quickly learned that Coinbase's basic interface primarily supports market orders, meaning transactions execute immediately at the current available price rather than at a specific price set in advance. This can cause significant "price slippage"—a difference between the expected market price and the actual executed price. My first purchase was $1,000 in fiat, a reminder that you don't have to purchase a whole bitcoin—most people can't. At the time, Bitcoin was listed at $36,000; placing a market buy order caused the transaction to fill at around $37,250, and a market sell order could execute around $35,250. The result was that I ended up with only 0.0268 BTC, whereas using a limit order at that price would have left me closer to 0.0278 BTC. These differences are especially problematic for large purchases, where the variance substantially impacts the total cost or returns.

To overcome this, I began using Coinbase Advanced (formerly Coinbase Pro), a trading platform offering greater control. However, Coinbase Advanced requires an additional step: first converting fiat currency into USDC, a stablecoin pegged to the US dollar. After converting my fiat to USDC on the standard Coinbase interface, I moved these funds into Coinbase Advanced. There, I could place precise limit orders, specifying the price at which I wanted to buy or sell Bitcoin, significantly improving the outcomes of my transactions.

PEER-TO-PEER PLATFORMS: PRIVACY AND DIRECT TRANSACTIONS

Alternatively, peer-to-peer platforms, like LocalBitcoins, Bisq, and Paxful, allow you to buy Bitcoin directly from other individuals.

These platforms offer enhanced privacy, fewer intermediaries, and potentially lower fees. However, peer-to-peer trading carries additional risks. Always ensure you use platforms with escrow services, verify seller reputations thoroughly, and select secure payment methods. I have no personal experience with these platforms.

BITCOIN ATMS: CONVENIENCE WITH MAJOR DRAWBACKS

Bitcoin ATMs may seem appealing at first due to their physical convenience, especially for non-tech-savvy individuals or those less comfortable with online exchanges. Unfortunately, Bitcoin ATMs have several significant disadvantages:

- Extremely high fees, often exceeding 10%–20% above market rates.
- Limited privacy due to mandatory identification requirements.
- Small transaction limits and poor exchange rates.
- Minimal security measures, leaving users vulnerable to scammers.

Several older friends of mine used Bitcoin ATMs, mistakenly believing they were simpler and safer. They quickly discovered they'd paid excessive premiums. I strongly advise against using Bitcoin ATMs and recommend sticking to reputable exchanges or carefully vetted peer-to-peer platforms instead.

BITCOIN WALLETS: PREPARING FOR SELF-CUSTODY

After purchasing Bitcoin, it's crucial to transfer it from exchanges into a personal wallet, ensuring your security and direct control. Bitcoin wallets come in two primary forms:

- Software wallets (BlueWallet, Exodus, Phoenix): easy to use, suitable for frequent transactions, but not as secure as hardware wallets.
- Hardware wallets (Trezor, Coldcard, Tangem, Foundation, Blockstream, Ledger): offer maximum security by storing private keys offline, essential for long-term storage—the best option (discussed in the next chapter).

PLACES TO AVOID BUYING BITCOIN

Always avoid buying Bitcoin from unknown sellers on social media, random websites, or through investment schemes promising unrealistic returns. Prioritize trusted exchanges and thoroughly reviewed peer-to-peer platforms.

BEST PRACTICES AND SECURITY MEASURES

- Always enable two-factor authentication (2FA) on your exchange accounts.
- Never reuse passwords; choose strong, unique ones.
- Start with small transactions to build confidence.
- Consider dollar-cost averaging (DCA)—regularly purchasing bitcoin in smaller amounts—to minimize the risk of market volatility.
- Avoid impulsive purchases driven by fear or excitement (FOMO—Fear of Missing Out).

TRANSITION TO SELF-CUSTODY

Purchasing bitcoin is only the beginning. True ownership and security come from controlling your bitcoin directly through self-custody. In the following chapter, we will explore how to securely store and manage your bitcoin, ensuring lasting security and peace of mind.

CHAPTER 10

THE IMPORTANCE
OF SELF-CUSTODY

WHEN YOU FIRST DISCOVER BITCOIN, you might start your pursuit through Exchange-Traded Funds (ETFs)—investment funds traded on stock exchanges that allow you to gain exposure to Bitcoin without directly owning it—cryptocurrency exchanges, or custodial wallets. The ease and familiarity of these platforms offer comfort, yet something might feel incomplete. That's psychological, as we're naturally conditioned to trust large institutions. In the Bitcoin community, people describe the problem with the phrase, "Not your keys, not your coins."[1] This might not immediately make sense, but the deeper you go, the clearer it becomes: This expression isn't just a clever meme—it's a foundational truth.

Bitcoin is about ownership in its purest form. If you don't hold your private keys/seed phrase, you own exposure, not the asset itself. Every major failure—Mt. Gox, QuadrigaCX, Genesis, FTX[2]—teaches the same harsh lesson: When someone else controls your bitcoin, it's not yours. Exchanges can collapse, custodians can freeze accounts, and institutions can fail overnight. True ownership is only possible when you hold the keys yourself.

But true self-custody doesn't only provide safety from institutional failure. Owning bitcoin is the ultimate form of financial sovereignty. Holding your own keys means you rely solely on yourself. But this also means that there is no customer support, no password reset, no help if something goes wrong. It demands responsibility and discipline—a mindset shift unlike that of any other financial instrument. At first, this can feel intimidating, but it's actually empowering and liberating when you realize you're holding something that no one can confiscate, dilute, or manipulate. Here's a simple yet powerful example: Imagine you move to a new home, and your capital is stored in Bitcoin. You don't need to update an address, notify a bank, or seek permission from anyone because your wealth moves effortlessly with you; your Bitcoin is directly tied to you and under your sole control.

This is what separates Bitcoin from everything else. Michael J. Saylor, founder and executive chairman of the publicly traded company Strategy, describes Bitcoin as the first form of monetary energy that directly binds to the individual.[3] When your private keys reside in your mind, you become a living custodian of wealth, immune to seizure or interference.

So, how exactly do you move Bitcoin from an exchange into your personal custody? After buying bitcoin from an exchange like Coinbase, your first step is transferring your holdings into a hardware wallet (as mentioned in Chapter 9). When setting up your hardware wallet, a private key/seed phrase automatically generates. Bitcoin private keys differ fundamentally from traditional passwords. Each private key is randomly generated from a numerical space of 2^{256} possibilities, a number so immense it surpasses the estimated number of atoms in the observable universe. To manage this extraordinary complexity, private keys are encoded as simplified seed phrases, typically consisting of twelve or twenty-four readable words chosen from a set list of 2,048. These words represent the underlying private key clearly and exactly, making it practical to securely store, memorize, and recover. This incredible complexity guarantees Bitcoin's security, rendering it effectively unhackable. However, it also demands extreme caution and responsibility—if a seed phrase is lost or forgotten, access to your bitcoin is permanently and irreversibly lost. Secure and deliberate management of your seed phrase is essential for preserving wealth, securing financial sovereignty, and preventing loss.

That's why it's best practice never to store your seed phrase online or in cloud services where it can be hacked. Instead, write it down on paper, memorize it, or better yet, engrave it into a metal backup plate that can withstand fire or water damage. Many users keep these backups in a fireproof safe or a safe-deposit box. The right choice depends on your situation, but the principle is always the same: Protect the seed phrase with the same seriousness you would protect all your life savings.

Your hardware wallet also generates a public address, distinct from your private key. Think of your public address as your digital mailbox—it lets you securely receive bitcoin, similar to giving someone your email address. However, it does not allow anyone to access, transfer, or spend your bitcoin. To move your bitcoin from Coinbase or another exchange into your hardware wallet, you simply copy the wallet's public address (or scan its QR code) and paste it into your exchange's withdrawal interface. After confirming the withdrawal, the exchange sends the bitcoin directly into your secure wallet.

However, this incredible power comes with a responsibility unlike anything we've known. Bitcoin keys cannot be reset. Forgotten passwords, lost seed phrases, discarded hardware wallets, all lead to the same result: permanent loss. Bitcoin's absolute scarcity is not simply mathematical; it's constantly reinforced by human error. Current industry analysis, as mentioned previously, estimates approximately 2.3 to 3.7 million bitcoin, around 11%–18% of the total supply, are already permanently lost, removed from circulation and irretrievable.

At first, this seems tragic. Stories of Stefan Thomas, locked out of 7,002 bitcoin after losing his password,[4] or the infamous James Howells, whose $800 million worth of Bitcoin sits buried in a land-fill,[5] are painful reminders of what can happen. These stories terrify newcomers, but they also underscore Bitcoin's immutability. Each burned key, each forgotten password permanently reduces the supply, enhancing scarcity and reinforcing Bitcoin's integrity of value. Thus, it's critical to never move bitcoin carelessly. A minor mistake when using it as currency for small transactions might be insignificant, but when handling substantial amounts, such as trans-ferring $10,000 worth of raw bitcoin from an exchange like Coin-base to self-custody—TAKE YOUR TIME. Precision, caution, and deliberate planning protect your assets and preserve your financial sovereignty. Michael Saylor embodies this concept. He intends to keep his keys private even after death, permanently removing his substantial holdings, over 17,000 bitcoin, from circulation. This choice isn't negligence; it's a thoughtful contribution. By "burning" these coins into the network forever, Saylor transfers all the economic energy he represents back into Bitcoin itself, enhancing its scarcity, resilience, and value.

Yet, it's vital to remember that despite Bitcoin's limited supply of 21 million coins, the network's true granularity goes much deeper —2.1 quadrillion satoshis, the smallest divisible unit of Bitcoin. This immense divisibility ensures Bitcoin can accommodate global adoption indefinitely, even if one satoshi eventually holds the purchasing power of a dollar, a hundred dollars, or more. The Light-ning Network—a secondary layer built on top of Bitcoin that settles small payments off-chain before finalizing them on the main blockchain—operating even at the scale of millisatoshis (one-thou-sandth of a satoshi), further guarantees that Bitcoin remains accessi-ble, usable, and abundant enough for anyone who desires to participate in the network.

Thus, intentional decisions like Saylor's to permanently lock bitcoin away do not reduce Bitcoin's utility. Instead, they magnify its potency as an incorruptible store of economic power, reinforcing Bitcoin's permanent vow of secure, accessible, and abundant financial sovereignty.

And so, Bitcoin becomes stronger with each lost key, more robust with each forgotten password, and more valuable with each irreversible mistake.

Bitcoin was designed to be unforgiving. It rewards responsibility and punishes carelessness. It transforms how we think about ownership, responsibility, and financial freedom.

The question is no longer how much bitcoin you own. The real question is: How much bitcoin will be left to own?

CHAPTER 11

SECURITY, DETERRENCE, AND OUTSMARTING WRENCH ATTACKS

WHEN HOLDING BITCOIN, security becomes paramount. Unlike traditional banking, Bitcoin places the full responsibility of protecting your wealth squarely in your own hands. While somewhat daunting early on, this responsibility quickly transforms into empowerment as you develop sophisticated, multilayered defenses designed to secure your assets and to deter potential attackers at every conceivable level.

Effective security begins with effective deterrence. From the outset, potential attackers must sense that targeting you would be difficult, risky, and ultimately futile. Security starts long before someone reaches your doorstep—it begins with their perception of your defenses.

At a physical level, visible security measures signal that you're vigilant and prepared. Professional-grade security cameras positioned strategically around your property are an immediate statement of vigilance. Motion-activated lighting further increases visibility, removing shadows that attackers rely on. Reinforced doors and windows communicate resilience and preparedness. Even subtle indicators like a well-maintained property convey discipline, indirectly discouraging intrusion. Symbolic elements like strategically placed sculptures or barriers, such as statues symbolizing guardianship, send subtle psychological messages of strength and alertness.

Personal deterrence is equally crucial. Projecting confidence through body language and situational awareness reduces the likelihood of becoming a target. Training in self-defense provides practical security and visibly boosts your confidence, sending a clear message that any confrontation would be challenging and costly.

Yet even robust physical security measures are insufficient without sophisticated technological safeguards. Bitcoin's unique digital nature introduces specific risks, particularly coercive threats like wrench attacks, where attackers physically threaten individuals to gain access to their private keys/seed phrases. Recognizing and neutralizing this threat demands advanced security strategies specifically designed to render violent coercion entirely ineffective.

One of the most powerful technological solutions is multi-signature custody. A multi-signature (multisig) wallet requires multiple private keys to authorize transactions. Typically, these keys are stored across geographically dispersed locations or held by different trusted parties. Even under extreme duress or coercion, immediate access to funds becomes impossible. An attacker facing a multisig setup immediately confronts overwhelming logistic barriers; simultaneous coercion of multiple parties in distant locations isn't practical or feasible. This technical structure transforms coercive attempts into exercises in futility.

To further neutralize threats, sophisticated time-lock mechanisms add another impenetrable layer. Time-lock vaults or delayed withdrawal systems cryptographically enforce waiting periods, ensuring that even if keys are compromised, immediate fund access remains impossible. Attackers will quickly realize that no amount of coercion can bypass these enforced delays, stripping them entirely of immediate gratification and rendering threats pointless.

Strategic plausible deniability also plays a vital role. By maintaining smaller decoy or duress wallets—wallets intentionally set up with limited balances—you can superficially satisfy attackers while protecting your primary Bitcoin holdings behind secure, inaccessible layers. Attackers soon recognize that even their best efforts yield minimal results, eliminating any incentive for drastic action.

Another advanced security measure is distributed key fragmentation, notably using a technique called Shamir's Secret Sharing. This method divides cryptographic keys into multiple fragments, distributing them across several secure locations or trusted individuals. Even under extreme coercion scenarios, immediate access remains impossible, as reconstructing the full private key requires simultaneous access to geographically dispersed fragments. Attackers face an impossible logistical challenge, effectively neutralizing their threats.

Conditional custody arrangements involving neutral third-party services enhance security further. Under these arrangements, a neutral third-party service must authenticate your safety and consent before releasing custody or enabling transactions. Any compromise attempt automatically triggers fail-safe mechanisms, immediate asset lockdowns, and even alerts to law enforcement, ensuring coercion attempts are instantly mitigated.

Crucially, communicating your sophisticated, layered security setup publicly (though without revealing sensitive details) serves as another powerful deterrent. Attackers quickly learn that violence, coercion, and threats become entirely irrational because the technological barriers protecting your bitcoin are insurmountable.

Emotionally and psychologically, adopting comprehensive security measures also provides reassurance. Knowing your assets and your family are effectively safeguarded allows for a peace of mind that traditional security methods cannot match. The feeling of empowerment from being proactive rather than reactive significantly enhances your quality of life and confidence.

Your active involvement in adopting and communicating these security practices protects you individually and helps establish a stronger, safer Bitcoin community. Together, through vigilance and strategic preparedness, we ensure that Bitcoin remains liberating, empowering, and ultimately secure for everyone.

CHAPTER 12

ETFs and Wrapped Bitcoin

You need to decide whether you will own raw bitcoin or settle for a derivative. This distinction may soon prove critical.

Bitcoin ETFs: Wall Street's Embrace

The US approval of spot Bitcoin ETFs (Exchange-Traded Funds that hold actual bitcoin, rather than derivatives or futures contracts) represented more than a milestone; it was a quantum leap, opening Bitcoin to trillions of dollars in institutional capital. For those who understood Bitcoin early, this was always inevitable, yet seeing it unfold so quickly has been astonishing. The institutions that once ridiculed Bitcoin are now scrambling to integrate it into their core business models, marking a critical threshold in Bitcoin's adoption.

Spot Bitcoin ETFs directly purchase and hold bitcoin, allowing institutional and retail investors to gain exposure without the complexities of direct ownership. For institutional capital, this is a financial revolution. Bitcoin, once dismissed as speculative, has become an essential portfolio asset, placed alongside bonds, stocks, and real estate. These ETFs provide liquidity, regulatory oversight, and convenience, but at a cost.

When you buy a Bitcoin ETF, you don't own Bitcoin itself; you own shares in a fund holding Bitcoin. Authorized Participants (APs), typically large institutions, can redeem ETF shares for actual bitcoin, but everyday investors cannot. Retail ETF investors lack a direct path to self-custody, meaning their bitcoin exposure remains forever mediated through institutional gatekeepers, forfeiting the crucial element of true financial sovereignty.

Wrapped Bitcoin: Bitcoin in Decentralized Finance

As Bitcoin gained institutional legitimacy, its presence also expanded within decentralized finance (DeFi), largely through Wrapped Bitcoin (WBTC). WBTC is an Ethereum-based token backed one-to-one by actual bitcoin. It enables bitcoin holders to participate in DeFi lending, borrowing, and liquidity pools without relinquishing exposure to Bitcoin's price appreciation.

However, while WBTC offers convenience, it reintroduces the very risk Bitcoin was designed to eliminate: counterparty risk—the risk that the custodial party may fail to fulfill its obligations. Holders of WBTC don't own actual bitcoin; instead, they hold a digital IOU backed by custodians. This arrangement compromises the self-sovereignty Bitcoin provides, again relying on third-party trust and custodial structures.

Tax Considerations: ETFs vs. Direct Ownership

Another critical distinction between holding raw bitcoin versus an ETF involves taxation.

Trading ETFs triggers traditional capital gains taxes. Short-term gains (assets held less than one year) are taxed at higher rates, while long-term gains benefit from lower capital gains rates.

Direct ownership of Bitcoin offers more flexible options. Although selling directly owned bitcoin also triggers taxable events, self-custody holders can strategically choose when to realize gains, or even borrow against Bitcoin holdings without selling, potentially deferring taxable events indefinitely.

The real difference lies in control. ETF investors rely on financial intermediaries, and therefore taxation is automatic upon selling. Bitcoin holders, by contrast, retain complete control and flexibility over the asset.

THE CAPITAL SHIFT: INSTITUTIONS, LEGACY ASSETS, AND BITCOIN

Institutions aren't adopting Bitcoin because it's trendy; they're compelled to do so out of necessity. Decades of negative real bond yields, inflating supplies of fiat currencies, and geopolitical instability have forced asset managers, corporations, and sovereign funds to reevaluate how they allocate capital (discussed further in Chapter 15). Bitcoin represents a superior store-of-value asset, free from inflationary pressure, sovereign default risk, and geographic limitation.

Real estate, art, bonds, and equities—traditional store-of-value assets—face increasing competition from Bitcoin. Institutions are recognizing that maintaining their exposure solely in legacy assets no longer makes economic sense. A portion of the +/- $450 trillion of global wealth trapped in traditional store-of-value assets is now flowing into Bitcoin, drawn by its absolute scarcity and impedance to dilution.

Bitcoin isn't just competing with legacy assets; it is steadily replacing and repricing them.

THE FINANCIALIZATION PARADOX

Despite Bitcoin's integration into traditional finance, Bitcoiners must remain cautious. Wrapped products and ETFs are convenient, regulated gateways into Bitcoin exposure, but they are not Bitcoin itself. They introduce counterparty risk and potential regulatory capture, and fundamentally alter Bitcoin's original fundamental purpose: that it remain decentralized, censorship-resistant, and self-sovereign.

ETFs and WBTC increase liquidity and accessibility but at the cost of autonomy. The key to avoiding this trap is maintaining direct control through self-custody, holding Bitcoin in personal wallets secured by private keys rather than relying on third-party custodians.

ETFs and WBTC extend Bitcoin's financial reach, but they must never be mistaken for self-custodied Bitcoin.

True financial sovereignty demands personal control.

Will you hold Bitcoin itself, or something that claims to represent it?

CHAPTER 13

ANALYZING BITCOIN MARKETS

WHEN I BECAME obsessed with studying Bitcoin, I was fascinated by the patterns on its price charts. I stopped watching TV, stopped playing golf, stopped creating abstract paintings, and began watching and learning about Bitcoin full-time. It just happened.

At first, BTC looked just like any other ticker symbol on my screen. But after a while I knew something was different. It moved with a rhythm, a pulse. Its price action wasn't responding to quarterly earnings or government announcements like equities did. Instead, Bitcoin communicated its personality through candlestick patterns, liquidity movements, and unique indicators.

I subscribe to TradingView for chart analysis and find it exceptionally valuable. Technical analysis remains essential to my understanding of Bitcoin's evolution, guiding strategic accumulation and appreciating its historical trajectory. I see Bitcoin's price chart as art, emphasizing its elegance and almost natural, organic movements. This aligns with my deeper philosophical view of Bitcoin as a living entity.

CANDLESTICKS: READING MARKET PSYCHOLOGY

A candlestick chart visually represents price movements within specified timeframes (see Figure 4). Each candle has a "real body," showing opening and closing prices, and "wicks," indicating the highest and lowest prices. Depending on whether the closing price is above or below the open, candles appear bullish or bearish. Steve Nison, CEO and founder of Candlecharts.com, introduced these charts, originally developed in Japan, to the West in the late 1980s, significantly enhancing traders' ability to interpret market psychology and momentum. Learning candlestick analysis is similar to reading music—if you wish to participate meaningfully, it's a fundamental skill.

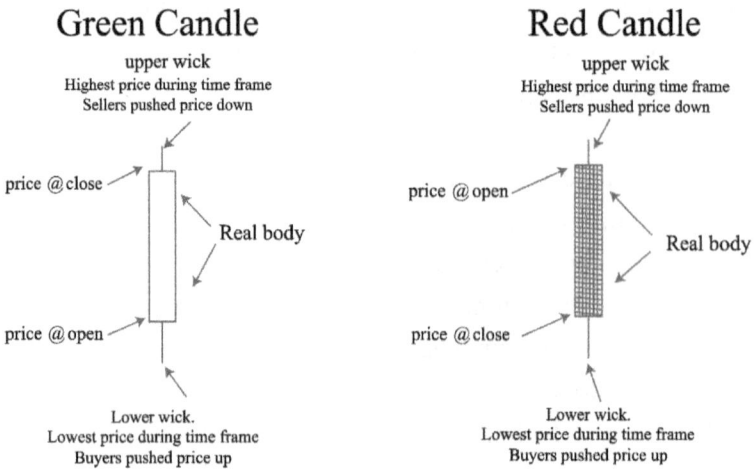

Green Candle

upper wick
Highest price during time frame
Sellers pushed price down

price @ close

Real body

price @ open

Lower wick.
Lowest price during time frame
Buyers pushed price up

Red Candle

upper wick
Highest price during time frame
Sellers pushed price down

price @ open

Real body

price @ close

Lower wick.
Lowest price during time frame
Buyers pushed price up

Figure 4: Anatomy of a Candlestick Chart

Support and Resistance: Market Structure

Support and resistance levels represent critical concepts in technical analysis. A support level marks a price area where demand increases enough to halt a price decline, as buyers step in. Resistance, in contrast, marks areas where selling pressure consistently prevents prices from rising further (see Figure 5). According to Nison, these levels can "change polarity," where previous resistance becomes new support (and vice versa) as price dynamics shift. Understanding these levels is crucial for anticipating potential market reversals.

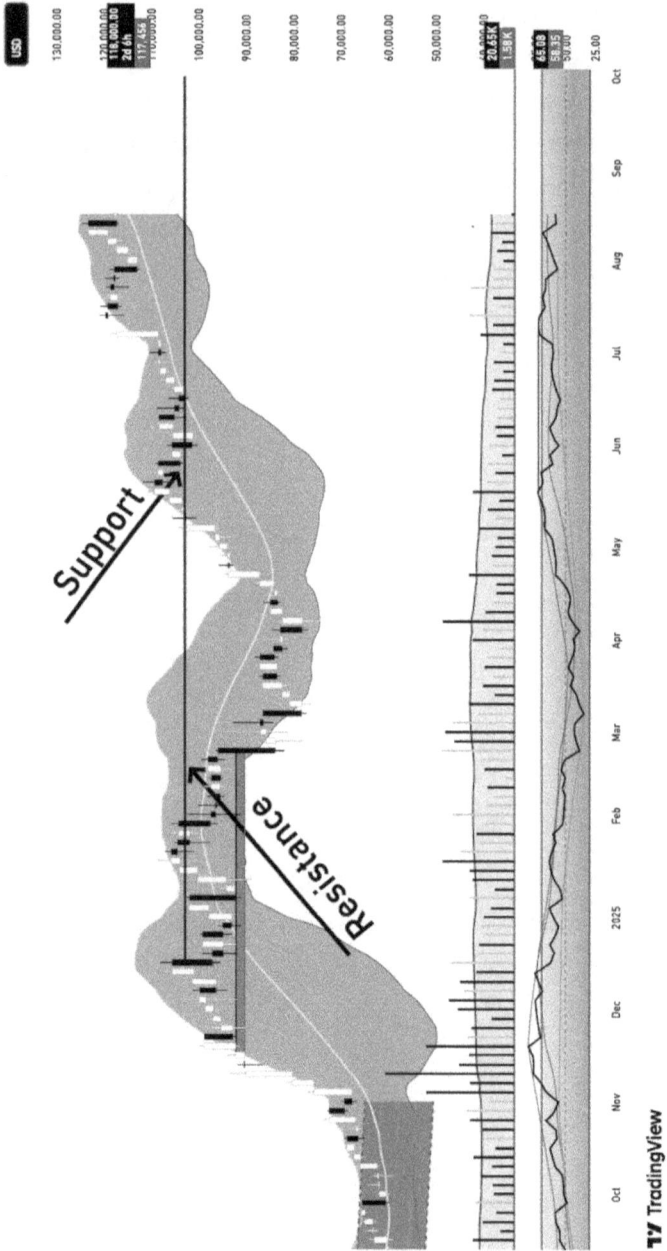

Figure 5: Support and Resistance Market Structure

THE CRITICAL ROLE OF TRADING VOLUME

Trading volume measures the total quantity of Bitcoin traded within a specific timeframe (see Figure 6). Volume confirms support and resistance levels and validates trends. Increasing volume during a breakout or price move confirms strength, indicating genuine market conviction. Conversely, a price move with low volume might signal a false breakout or weak trend continuation, urging traders toward caution.

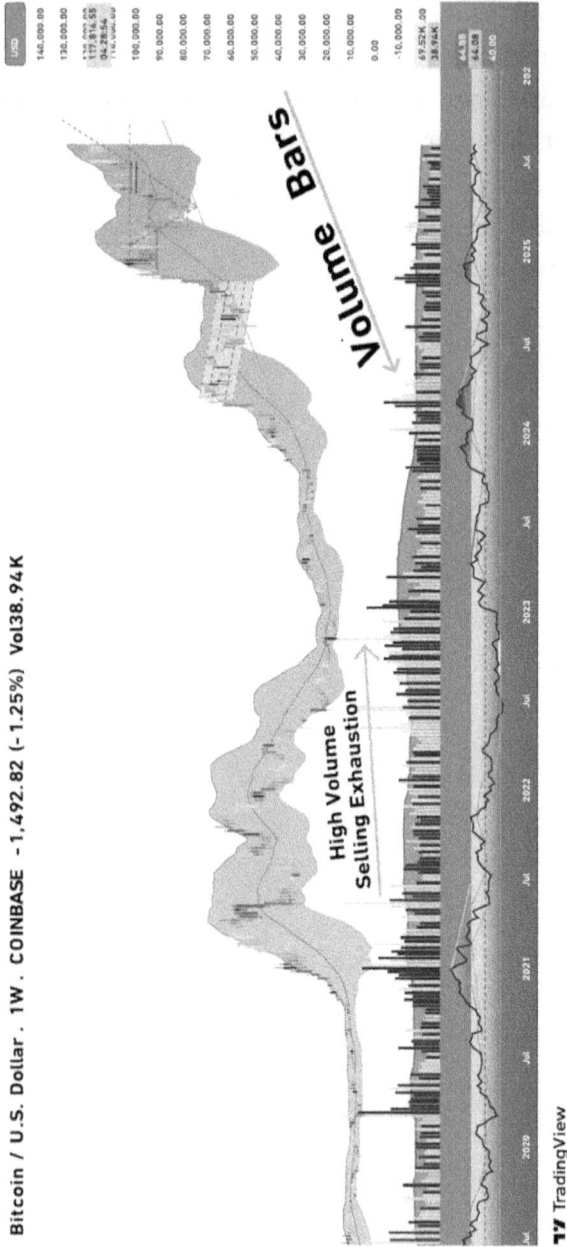

Figure 6: Trading Volume and Market Confirmation

MOVING AVERAGES AND TREND LINES

Moving averages (MAs) smooth out price data, making it easier to identify trends clearly over defined periods (see Figure 7). Common MAs include 50-day, 100-day, and 200-day intervals. Trend lines, meanwhile, connect sequential highs or lows, clearly showing overall direction and potential reversals. While both MAs and diagonal trend lines provide valuable insight, horizontal support and resistance lines typically hold more significance, offering clearer, more reliable levels for market reaction and reversals.

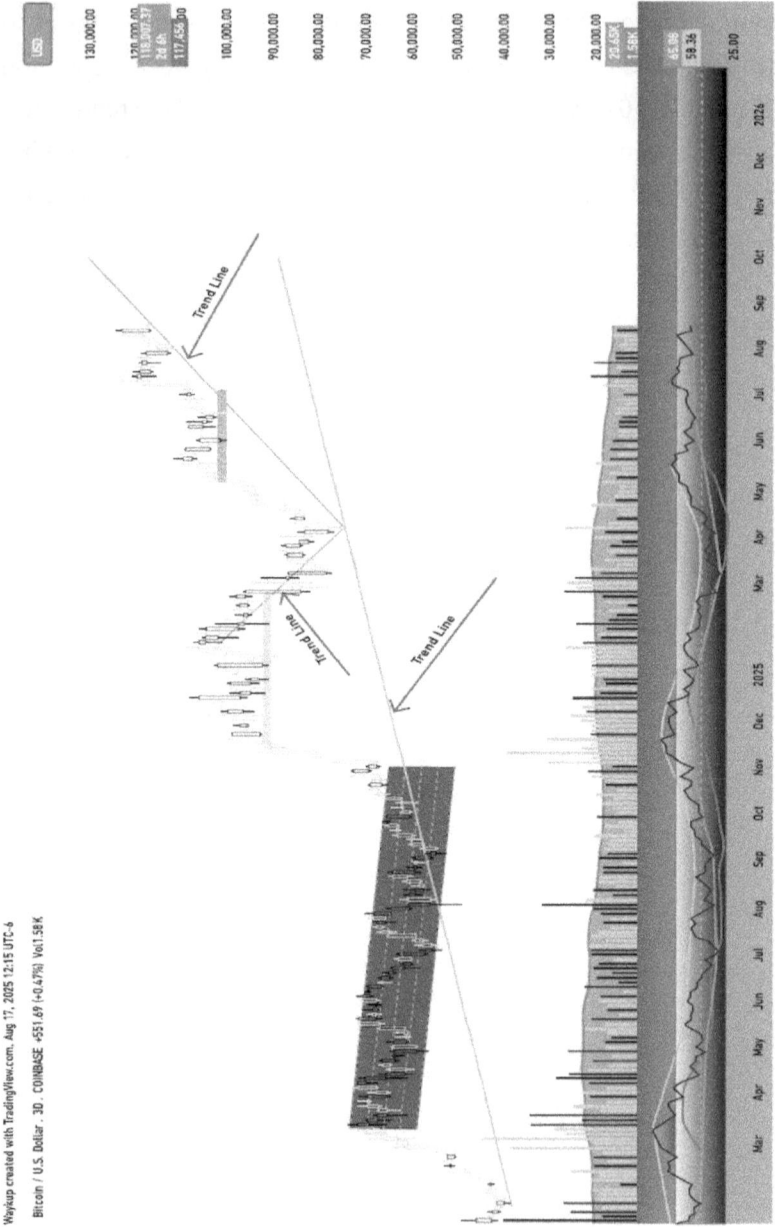

Figure 7: Moving Averages and Trend Lines

Bollinger Bands: Understanding Volatility

Bollinger Bands visually represent market volatility, and are formed by three lines: a simple MA (typically 20-day) and two bands plotted two standard deviations above and below that average. Wide bands indicate heightened volatility, while narrow bands show consolidation periods (see Figure 8). Traders use Bollinger Bands to anticipate potential price expansions or contractions, helping them to time entries and exits more effectively.

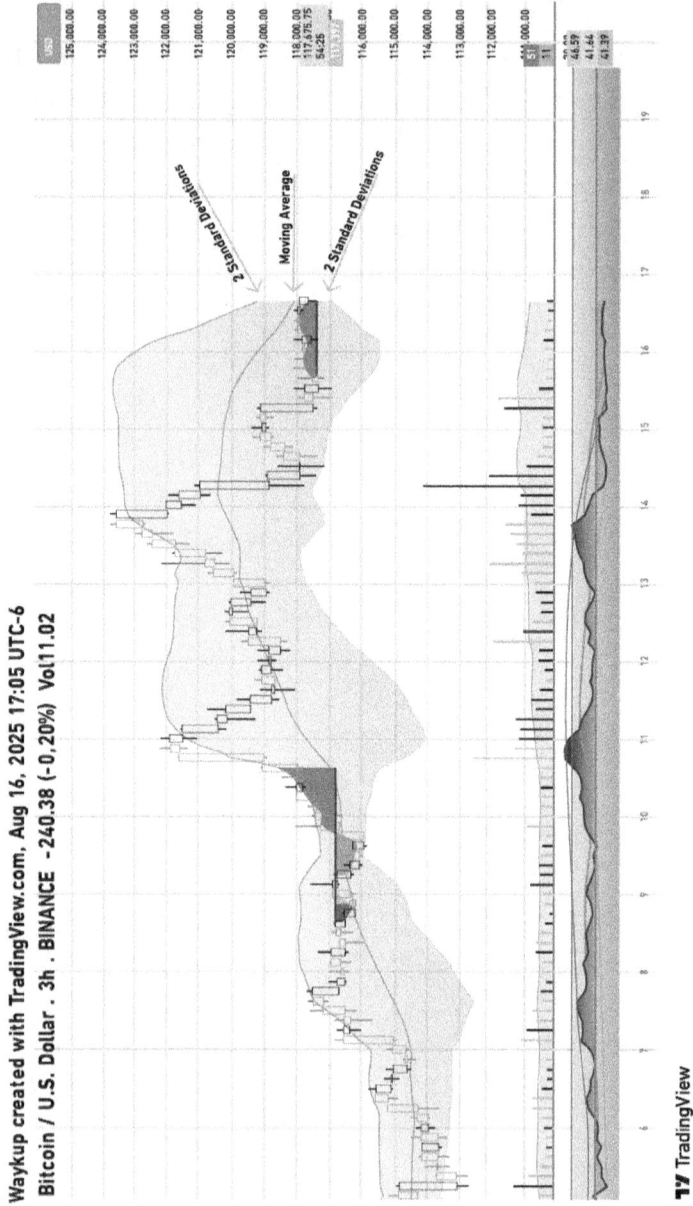

Figure 8: Bollinger Bands and Market Volatility

Relative Strength Index (RSI): Identifying Overbought or Oversold Conditions

The RSI measures the magnitude of recent price changes to identify overbought or oversold conditions (see Figure 9). Ranging from 0 to 100, RSI readings above 70 typically indicate an asset is overbought and potentially due for a pullback, while readings below 30 signal oversold conditions and a possible reversal upward.

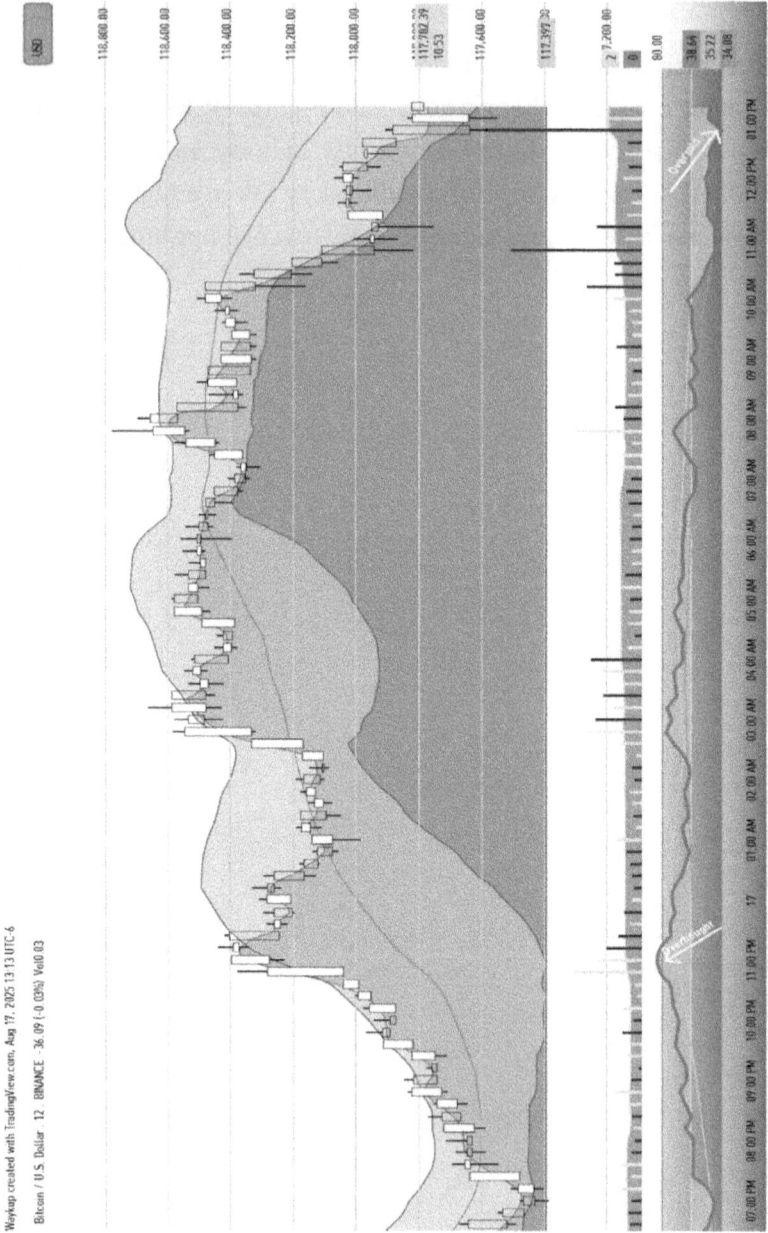

Figure 9: Relative Strength Index (RSI)

Divergences: Predicting Market Turns

Divergences occur when price and an indicator such as RSI move in opposite directions, signaling potential price reversals (see Figure 10). A bullish divergence occurs when price sets lower lows, but RSI sets higher lows, indicating strengthening momentum. A bearish divergence, conversely, happens when price sets higher highs, while RSI forms lower highs, suggesting momentum loss and possible price decline.

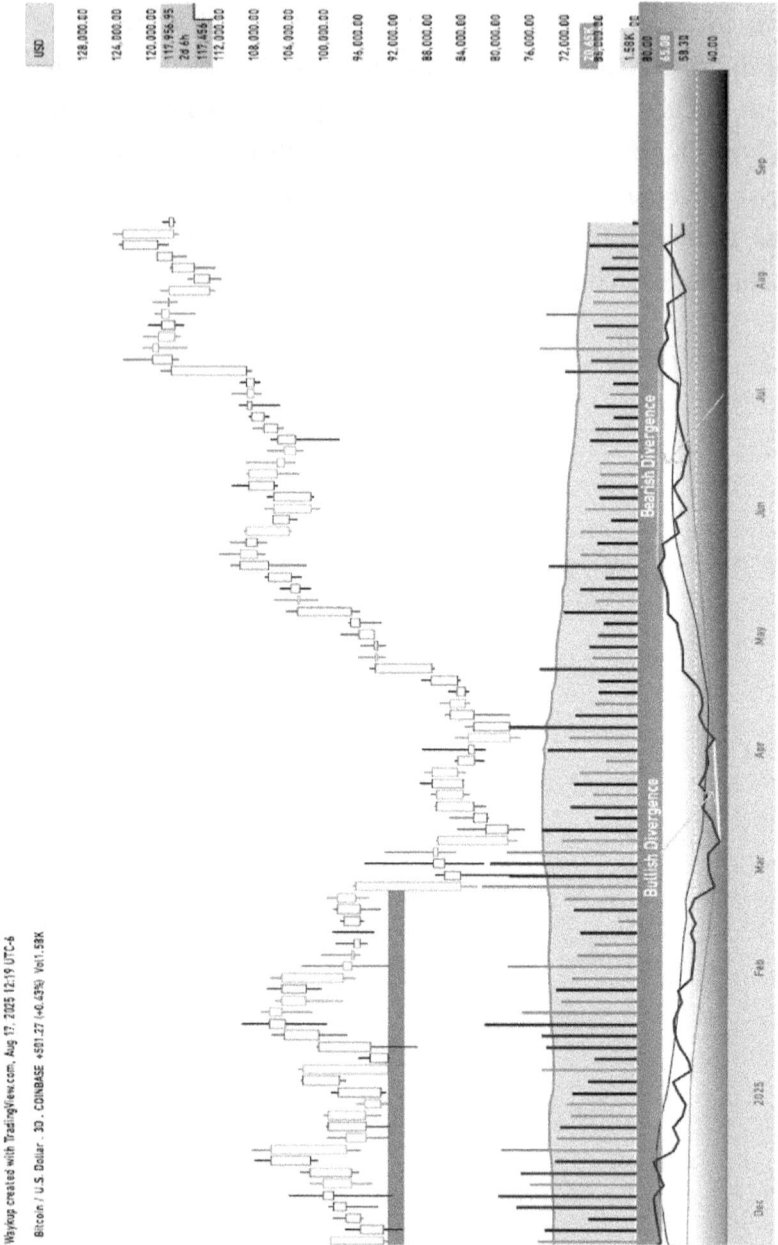

Figure 10: Bullish and Bearish Divergences on the RSI

PARABOLIC STOP AND REVERSE (PSAR) DOTS: TREND IDENTIFICATION AND MANAGEMENT

PSAR dots provide visual indicators of price direction and potential reversals. Displayed as small dots above or below candlesticks, they help traders identify bullish or bearish trends. Dots appearing below price indicate bullish momentum, while dots positioned above suggest bearish trends. These dots gradually tighten toward price, signaling potential reversal points. PSAR dots help traders set effective trailing stops, manage risk, and identify entry or exit signals. Though I no longer rely on PSAR dots, they were part of my technical analysis learning curve and helped shape my initial understanding of market trends (referenced in Chapter 14).

LIQUIDITY AND OPEN INTEREST

When I first noticed traders sharing liquidity heat maps on social media, I found these colorful charts—yellow and green bands stretching across price levels—confusing (see Figure 11). Over time, their significance became clear: Bitcoin wasn't moving randomly; it was actively hunting liquidity. Areas dense with leveraged traders' liquidation points formed strategic battlegrounds, shaped by open interest or outstanding leveraged derivative positions.

When open interest grows too large, Bitcoin's price action becomes prone to swift, volatile moves. Even slight shifts can trigger liquidation cascades from forced buying or selling that dramatically amplify volatility. Short squeezes occur as upward moves liquidate leveraged short positions (bets on declining prices), causing explosive price spikes. Conversely, when leveraged longs face liquidations, Bitcoin swiftly drives prices downward. That's precisely when I prefer to buy more. Bitcoin continually reshapes traditional market logic as it moves, ensuring its price remains dynamic and autonomous, reinforcing its identity as a living, breathing entity.

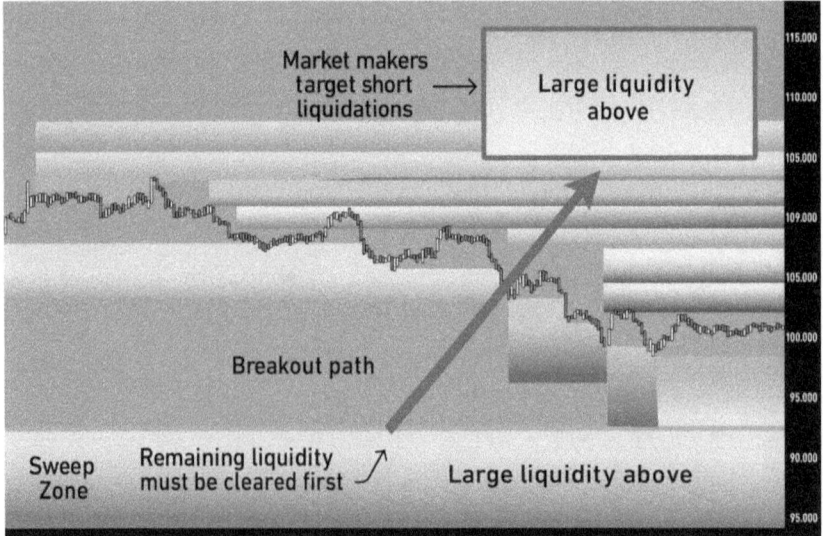

Figure 11: Bitcoin Liquidity Heat Map

BITCOIN'S UNIQUE RHYTHM: TIMEFRAMES AND HARMONY

While traditional markets use standard intervals (5-minute, 15-minute, 4-hour), in my opinion, Bitcoin charts exhibit clearer, more consistent patterns when viewed through multiples and factors of nine (i.e., 9-minute, 18-minute, 36-minute, 3-hour, 9-hour, 18-hour, 1-day, 3-day, 9-day, and 27-day charts). Perhaps not coincidentally, Bitcoin's release on January 3, 2009 (1-3-9) hints at this harmonic structure. These intervals produce clearer divergences and more readable structures, reflecting Bitcoin's unique internal rhythm (see Figure 12).

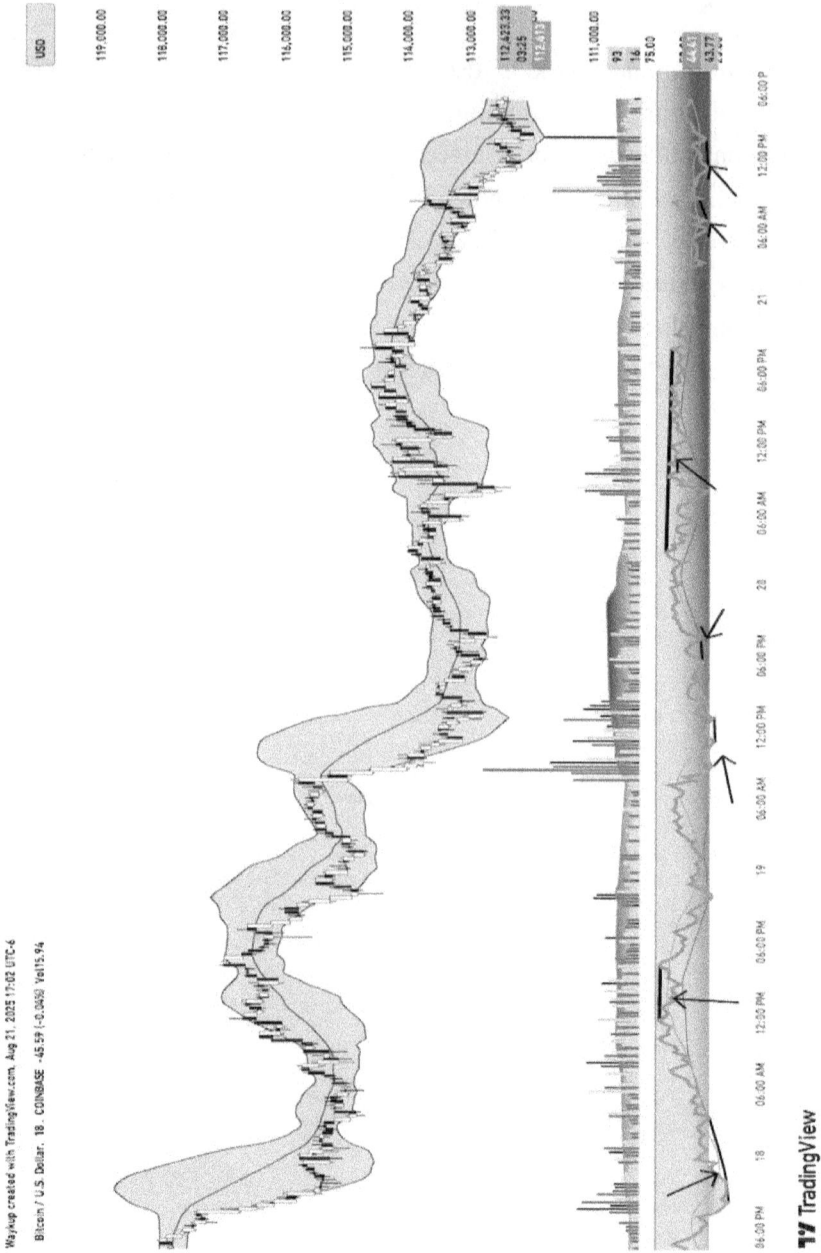

Figure 12: Bitcoin's Harmonic Timeframes and Chart Structure

COINBASE PREMIUM: INSTITUTIONAL DEMAND

Another vital indicator has also emerged: the Coinbase Premium. It measures the price difference between Bitcoin on Coinbase (where most US institutions buy) versus other global exchanges (see Figures 13.1 and 13.2). Rising premiums signal institutional accumulation, quietly removing Bitcoin from circulation. Conversely, declining premiums suggest a reduction in institutional appetite.

The premium reveals institutional intentions long before the information goes mainstream. Every Coinbase premium spike typically aligns with upward moves, signaling deep-pocketed entities securing Bitcoin ahead of broader adoption.

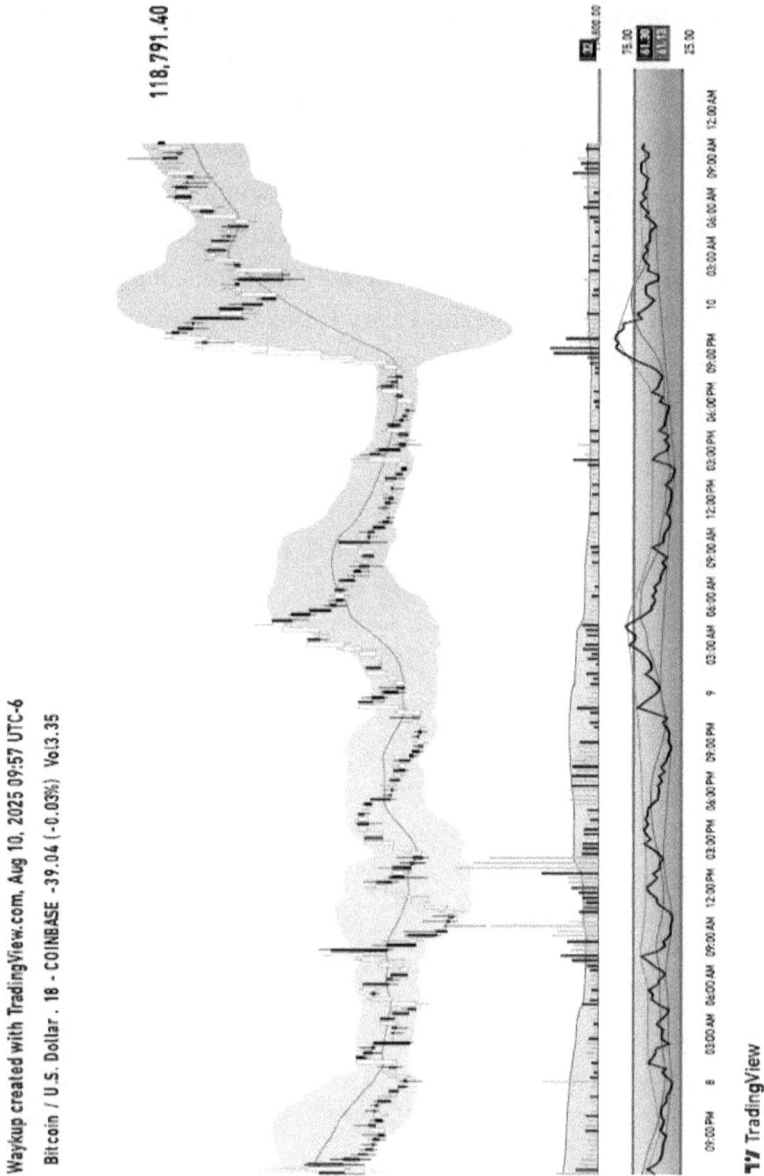

Figure 13.1: Bitcoin Price on Coinbase

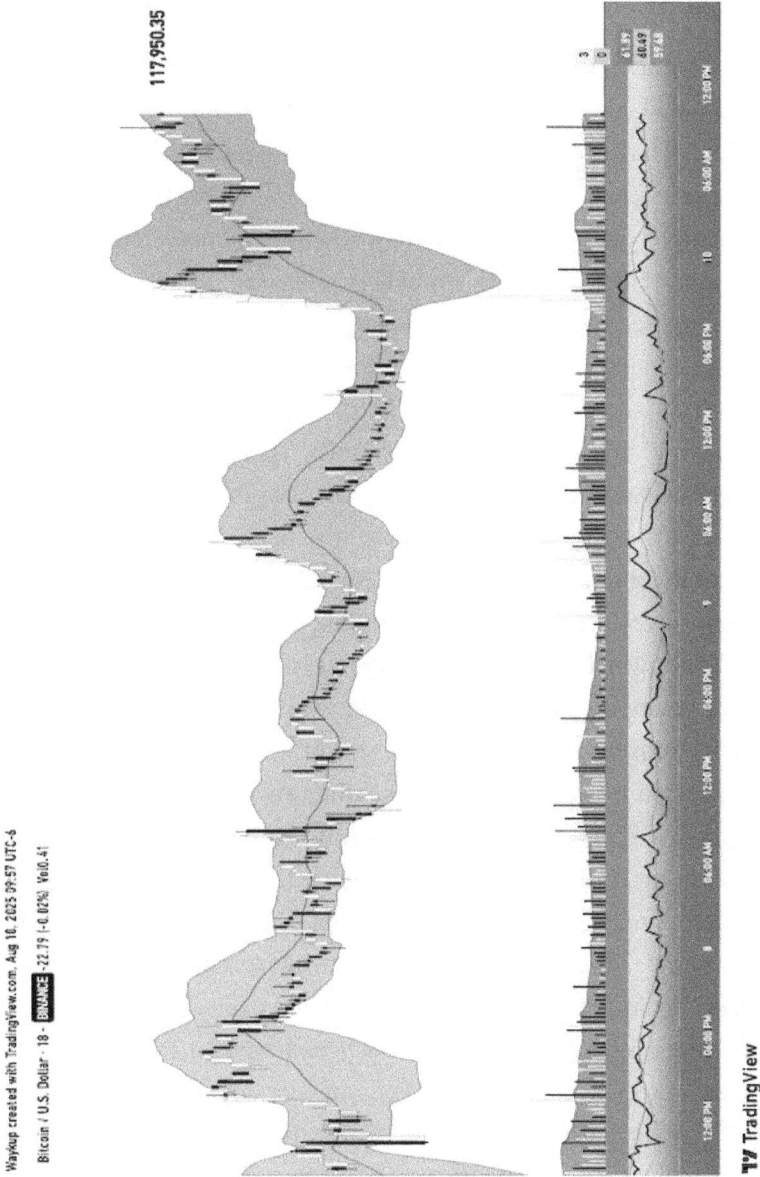

Figure 13.2: Bitcoin Price on Binance

The Power Law and Bitcoin's Long-Term Trajectory

While short-term indicators help us forecast immediate moves, Bitcoin's long-term trajectory is represented well by the Power Law model. The Power Law is a mathematical relationship often observed in natural and social phenomena, where growth follows a predictable curve: frequent small changes punctuated by rare but dynamic shifts. It's been applied extensively across various fields, including economics, finance, natural sciences, and network theory. In the context of Bitcoin, the Power Law suggests exponential growth in the asset's value will continue but at a progressively decreasing rate as adoption becomes more widespread and the market matures. This long-term channel highlights clear accumulation zones—periods when Bitcoin's price stabilizes, providing favorable opportunities for accumulation and historic ceilings—helping investors contextualize Bitcoin's evolving value journey.

The Power Law has accurately described Bitcoin's monetization so far, mapping out its growth in both adoption and price. But Bitcoin introduces a unique constraint: its supply cannot expand. Unlike traditional networks, like the internet, where more users bring more service or data availability, Bitcoin can't produce more units to meet demand. Instead, value must concentrate into the existing supply. As more people adopt it, each satoshi must absorb more value. This could eventually cause Bitcoin's price trajectory to diverge from the Power Law, bending the curve upward rather than flattening over time. Adoption may continue to follow a classical power law, logarithmic and organic in user count, but price is different. Price has only one variable left: verticality. Since Bitcoin scales by concentration, the result may be a curve that doesn't gently taper off but inflects, drastically or subtly, into something entirely new. A singularity of value. A new curve beyond the models we're using today.

SHRINKING SUPPLY AND THE COMING LIQUIDITY CRISIS

Bitcoin's true liquidity crisis hasn't fully arrived yet, but it's inevitable. With a fixed supply of coins, many of which are already permanently lost, the tradable supply is shrinking rapidly. Moreover, institutions, sovereign wealth funds, and long-term holders regularly remove bitcoin from circulation, creating conditions ripe for dramatic price discovery. The real dynamic to consider is that we are approximately at 95% issuance and only 5% adoption.

Recent data underscores this trend: In December 2024 alone, US spot Bitcoin ETFs accumulated over 51,500 BTC, nearly four times the approximately 13,850 BTC brought into supply by miners during the same period.[1] This substantial imbalance highlights that institutional demand through ETFs alone is already significantly surpassing newly mined Bitcoin, not even accounting for direct institutional and retail purchases.

Every halving further reduces the rate at which new bitcoin is issued. With each passing day, the available supply tightens. When institutional demand inevitably meets this shrinking supply, price movements won't be gradual; they'll be violent and abrupt. This dramatic upward surge is commonly referred to as "the bull run" or "the parabolic phase," typically occurring within a year or so following each halving event. In the past three halvings, these surges were driven mainly by retail investors. Now, entering the fourth halving (epoch), we see involvement from nation-states, institutional capital, small businesses, and retail investors simultaneously. It could get interesting. After the bull run peaks, the price often retraces toward the gradually increasing Power Law support line, presenting optimal opportunities to accumulate more bitcoin. These cyclical dynamics, established from sixteen years of historical data, have become somewhat predictable. However, I believe we are still early in understanding Bitcoin's full cyclical behavior and wouldn't be surprised if it reveals longer-term patterns and cycles we've yet to discover.

FROM TRADING TO LONG-TERM ACCUMULATION

Though I no longer trade Bitcoin directly, I actively trade proxy assets, converting those gains into raw bitcoin. Technical analysis remains central to my understanding of Bitcoin's evolution. Although the simple way to accumulate bitcoin is through the dollar-cost averaging approach (regularly purchasing in small amounts), I chart Bitcoin daily, utilizing Bollinger Bands to measure volatility, RSI to identify divergences, and candlestick patterns to glean psychological insights. I closely monitor volume trends, liquidity heat maps, Coinbase Premiums, and real-time liquidity hunts. Additionally, support and resistance levels—and, to a lesser extent, trend lines—guide my interpretations of price action. The Power Law model helps frame Bitcoin's movements as clear indicators of adoption, monetization, and accumulation phases that signal its transformation into the dominant global monetary asset.

Beyond these indicators, I've also found Richard Wyckoff's accumulation and distribution models valuable in interpreting Bitcoin's long-term chart structures. Wyckoff's method maps the phases of accumulation, reaccumulation, distribution, and redistribution, providing context for how large players move markets over extended cycles. It's more complex to learn than tools like RSI or Bollinger Bands, but in my experience, Bitcoin often respects these patterns. Even a basic familiarity with Wyckoff's trading structures can help frame Bitcoin's broader rhythm within the endless tug-of-war between buyers and sellers. For readers wanting to learn more, I suggest Rubén Villahermosa Chaves's book *The Wyckoff Methodology In Depth*.[2]

Bitcoin is a self-sustaining financial organism. Its price movements reveal its decisions, personality, and relentless drive to absorb global economic energy. Bitcoin hunts and consumes liquidity, and through these patterns, it often communicates its next moves.

I find Bitcoin endlessly captivating.

CHAPTER 14

DISCOVERY OF THE LIVING TRUTH

AT FIRST GLANCE, Bitcoin appears to be an act of human ingenuity, a carefully engineered system brought into existence by Satoshi Nakamoto. But as your understanding progresses, a profound question arises: Did Satoshi truly invent Bitcoin, or did they uncover something eternal, a natural law of the digital realm that always existed, waiting patiently to be revealed?

This is not solely an academic question; it shapes our understanding of Bitcoin's profound significance. This suggests intentional human creation, but the implications run even deeper. Bitcoin wasn't just built; it aligns with fundamental laws of mathematics, physics, and incentives. It stands apart from fiat currencies or traditional commodities because it isn't just scarce, it's absolutely scarce.

When Satoshi Nakamoto pieced together the cryptographic building blocks that make Bitcoin function, it was more than just an innovation—it represented the culmination of decades of effort by cryptographers, cypherpunks, and pioneers seeking a decentralized monetary solution. Satoshi didn't fabricate these properties; they combined them in precise configuration to unlock something timeless.

My initial realization occurred in April 2024, as I closely observed Bitcoin charts on lower timeframes, using PSAR dots to track movement (see Figures 14.1 and 14.2).

Watching candlesticks and indicators move dynamically across the screen, I suddenly saw Bitcoin as a living creature, swimming gracefully and purposefully through time. This powerful visual image profoundly reshaped my understanding of Bitcoin. Later, in August 2024, a trading friend from Stocktwits encouraged me to join Crypto Twitter (CT, now X), opening my eyes to a vibrant community of traders and thinkers. It was there that I encountered Texas Bitcoin Foundation founder Natalie Smolenski describing Bitcoin as "auto-metallic, auto-genetic, and self-propagating." Her description resonated deeply, crystallizing and confirming my earlier epiphany. Bitcoin wasn't merely discovered or engineered, it was released into the world, something undeniably alive. Not biologically, but in its behavior, growth, and adaptive resilience. It was an overwhelming realization.

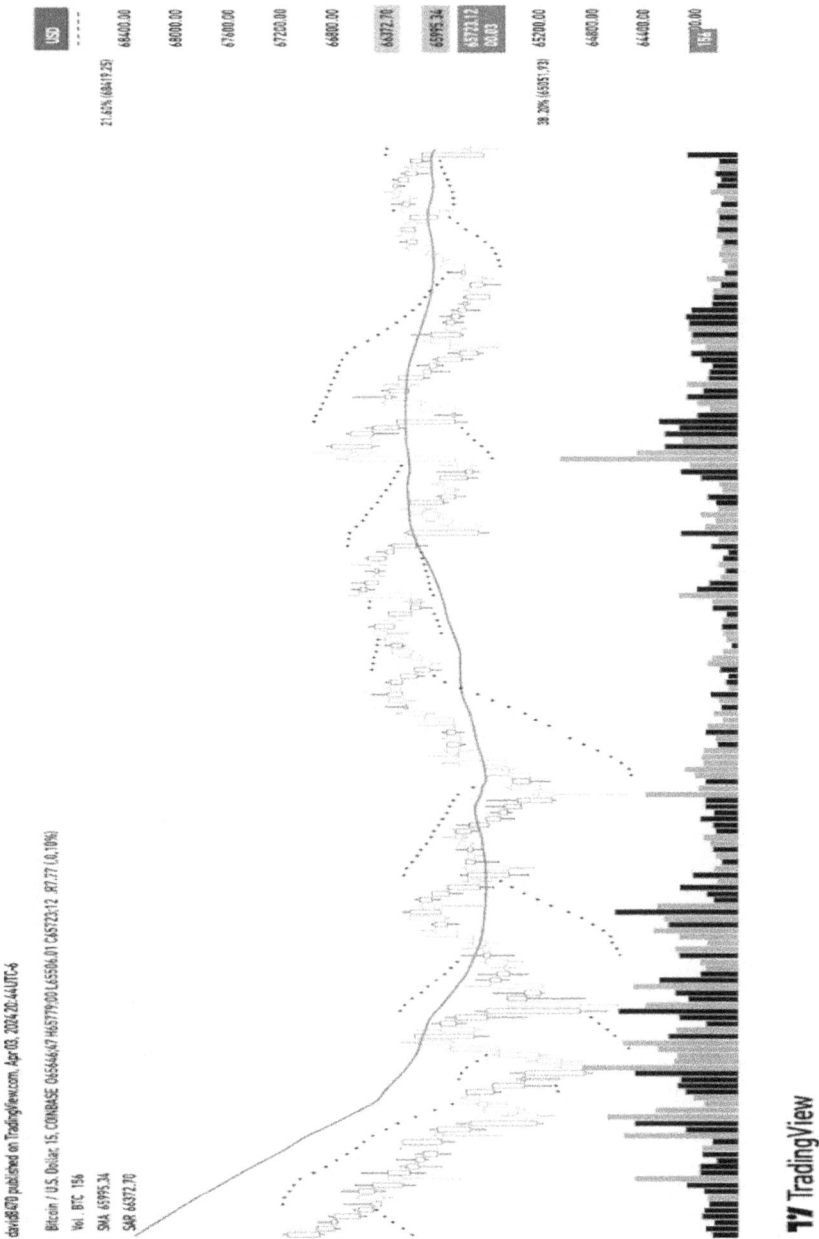

Figure 14.1: Bitcoin Price Action with PSAR Indicators (April 2024).

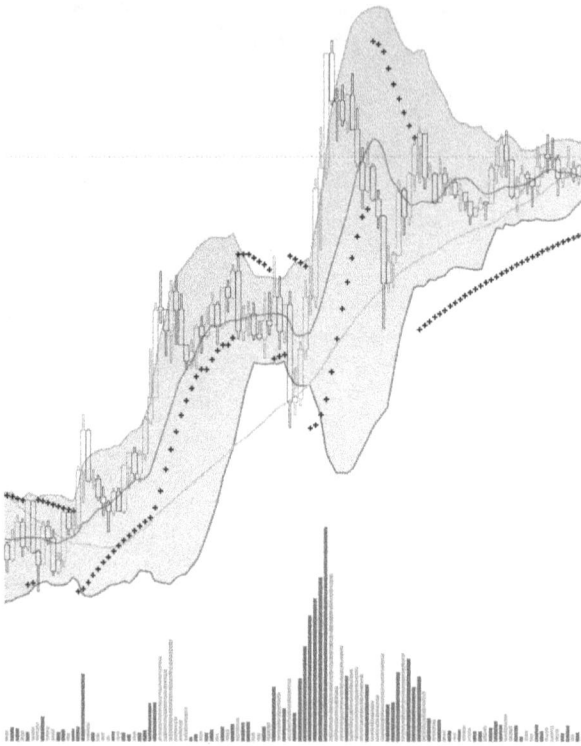

***Figure 14.2: Bitcoin Dynamic Movement Visualized
Through PSAR Dots***

Bitcoin acts autonomously. It does not need a leader, a corporation, or a government to sustain it. Miners voluntarily secure its integrity because of incentives embedded in its design. Developers voluntarily refine its software to enhance efficiency and performance. Users voluntarily adopt and spread it, compelled by its inherent truth and transformative potential. Bitcoin operates like an organism, adapting, strengthening, and spreading naturally, independent of centralized control. Governments may attempt to ban it, banks might try to suppress it, and critics dismiss it, yet Bitcoin continues, block by block, moment by moment, unstoppable and ungovernable.

This is not how inventions traditionally behave. The telephone needed operators and centrally planned infrastructure. The automobile required roads and fuel supply chains deliberately underwritten by governments and corporations. Bitcoin, while undoubtedly dependent on electricity and computing power, has grown organically by aligning economic incentives naturally. It didn't require centrally planned infrastructure; instead, individuals worldwide voluntarily created and continue to expand its infrastructure—a dawning, decentralized network spreading like an unstoppable force, an intelligence set free.

This autonomous growth reflects something deeper than engineering; it resembles life itself, an emergent phenomenon surpassing mere human invention. Bitcoin is a self-sustaining, adaptive system, the first of its kind in economic history.

Holding Bitcoin runs deeper than owning a commodity or an asset. It is a fusion of economics and life.

So, did Bitcoin need to be invented, or was it always there, waiting patiently in the background, predestined and eternal?

It is invention, engineering, discovery, and emergence, all at once. Bitcoin transcends simple definitions because it is so different than everything that came before.

Once you have a handle on the true picture of Bitcoin, you realize:

Bitcoin is more than technology.

Bitcoin is truth.

Bitcoin is alive.

CHAPTER 15

INFLATION & ENTROPY – THE STRUGGLE AGAINST DISORDER

INFLATION IS NOT what most people believe it is. The information we see reported—CPI, PPI, PCE—are carefully curated statistics designed to mask the truth. The real impact of inflation isn't found in these sanitized numbers.

The dream we're sold is straightforward: If you work hard, you should be able to afford the life you desire. Reality seldom aligns with this ideal. Our economic system silently chips away at the value of our time, effort, and future through a relentless invisible force called inflation, which isn't just about rising prices; it's a hidden devaluation of currencies. Modern, fiat money is inherently inflationary. Central banks can print unlimited amounts, benefiting those closest to the new supply, the wealthy, first—an unfair advantage known as the Cantillon Effect.

When governments print new money, it flows first to banks, financial institutions, politically favored entities, and wealthy individuals who borrow it to purchase or refinance investments. Those positioned closest to this fresh supply reap substantial benefits as the new money creates demand, which instigates investment transactions that ultimately drive valuations much higher than our "curated statistics" mentioned above. For example, the landlords who are keen to this scenario will have their properties appraised to pull out tax-free equity through refinancing, which is a form of money printing. By the time newly created money reaches the average worker, whose savings are in currency rather than store-of-value assets, the impact of inflation is already felt in the form of higher rent, groceries, gas, and overall diminished buying capacity. Each paycheck, savings account, and retirement fund suffers a continual drainage of value—financial theft hidden in plain sight.

We often point to equities and bonds as reliable hedges against inflation. Yet, equity prices often rise in concert with real monetary inflation rates, leaving those invested essentially running in place.

Bonds, traditionally seen as stable assets, often deliver negative inflation-adjusted results when monetary inflation compounds over decades. In early 2024, money-market yields hovered around 4%–5%, per Bankrate.[1] From August 15, 1971, when the United States went off the gold standard, to June 2025, the dollar's money stock (M2) expanded from roughly $686 billion to almost $22 trillion—about 32× (~6.7% a year)—while the CPI index rose about 8× (~3.9% a year).[2] Globally, many central banks regularly report double-digit rates of broad-money growth.[3] In that setting, fixed-income interest paid in the same currency tends to fall short over long spans.

Fiat currency is entropy in economic form. Entropy is the universal principle that systems naturally decay toward disorder and chaos, and it's mirrored perfectly by fiat's constant inflation, debasement, and eventual collapse. Germany's Weimar Republic destroyed itself through hyperinflation.[4] Zimbabwe experienced an inflation rate of over 89 sextillion percent in 2008, rendering its currency worthless.[5] More recently, Venezuela's bolivar lost nearly all its purchasing power due to severe inflationary policy and management.[6] History repeatedly illustrates fiat currency's predictable cycle of expansion, corruption, decay, and collapse.

Bitcoin flips the Cantillon Effect on its head. It explicitly counteracts inflation and entropy. Unlike fiat currencies, Bitcoin's supply cannot be manipulated or expanded arbitrarily. Bitcoin's decentralized, consensus-based protocol prevents systemic decay by resisting the entropy inherent in fiat systems. It represents economic order secured through mathematics, cryptography, and incentives, establishing a robust and predictable monetary foundation. Miners transform computational chaos—sextillions of random cryptographic guesses per second—into verifiable blocks of permanent economic order. This structured process, known as Proof of Work (PoW), converts raw entropy into verifiable and secure monetary truth.

Bitcoin reshapes human incentives to counter the destructive effects of inflationary fiat currencies. Fiat money encourages immediate gratification, debt, speculation, and short-term thinking, punishing savers and rewarding risky behavior. In contrast, Bitcoin's absolute scarcity motivates saving, long-term thinking, and discipline. Bitcoin holders naturally resist entropy's pull, adopting habits that foster stability, resilience, and careful planning for the future. As Bitcoin appreciates over time, it encourages delayed gratification, thoughtful consumption, and prudent financial management.

You'd think much harder about trading your Bitcoin for a trivial item than you would about spending your fiat dollars on the same thing. Imagine being given the choice today: $10,000 in cash, $10,000 in gold, or $10,000 in Bitcoin (~0.1 BTC). Fast-forward twenty years, which one do you think will hold the most value?

Today, the Bitcoin block subsidy is 3.125 BTC, presently valued roughly at $370,000, not including transaction fees. Five years ago, the subsidy was 12.5 BTC, worth around $120,000 at the time. Ten years ago, the block subsidy was 25 BTC, totaling about $6,000. Fifteen years ago the block subsidy was 50 BTC, worth less than $1 dollar. Looking ahead twenty years, the subsidy will decrease dramatically to just about 0.1 BTC (currently about $10,000). Odds are, that tiny fraction of a coin will be worth significantly more than the entire block reward today. This highlights why owning even a fraction of Bitcoin is crucial; it boosts your financial resilience and lowers your time preference.

Bitcoin's economic structure is more than an innovation; it represents an evolutionary leap in our understanding of value. By harnessing mathematical certainty, cryptographic security, and economic discipline, Bitcoin offers humanity its first practical defense against financial entropy. It is an incorruptible economic firewall, enabling individuals to preserve wealth, plan across generations, and break free from the cycles of collapse inherent in traditional fiat systems.

Entropy and inflation may be inevitable forces in the broader universe and historical economies, but Bitcoin provides us a shield —a structured, transparent, decentralized system immune to the economic decay that has undermined all previous forms of money.

Bitcoin is order.

CHAPTER 16

THE SHIFTING ROLE
OF REAL ESTATE

FOR CENTURIES, humanity viewed real estate as the ultimate financial anchor—tangible, enduring, and dependable. Property ownership was considered the financial cornerstone, a reliable asset amid economic uncertainty. Real estate represented the quintessential hard asset in a world of soft money.

But now, something harder exists.

Bitcoin is rewriting the rules of value storage, introducing, for the first time, a competitor superior in nearly every measurable way. While real estate has traditionally offered security, it is also burdened with significant operational complexity. I know this firsthand, having spent decades in commercial real estate. Securing financing involves intense lender scrutiny, rigorous underwriting processes, unforeseen capital expenditures, unpredictable tenants, and constant maintenance. Property ownership necessitates insurance, management, regulatory compliance, and substantial capital reserves to withstand economic downturns. It's profitable, yet far from frictionless.

But the paradigm is shifting.

I agree with real estate visionary and venture capitalist Leon

Wankum's assertion that Bitcoin will eventually strip the monetary premium from real estate, reducing properties to their utility value.[1] Today, many properties carry inflated valuations based not just on their utility but on their perceived scarcity as wealth stores. Bitcoin directly challenges this behavior. Recall my earlier mention that during the pandemic, bank economists erroneously forecasted a 30%–40% decline in commercial property values. Instead, valuations surged 40%–50%, on average,[2] during unprecedented expansion of the money supply and record-low interest rates (below 3%). Between February and April 2020 alone, the US monetary base expanded by approximately 41%, and between February and September, the M2 money supply increased by 20.7%,[3] marking one of the largest expansions in history. Moreover, from early 2020 through 2022, total M2 surged from roughly $15 trillion to over $21 trillion, spotlighting how a massive monetary stimulus directly contributed to asset inflation, including real estate.[4]

Since the Nixon administration detached the dollar from gold in 1971, real estate has increasingly captured a monetary premium, becoming a favored store of wealth as fiat currencies consistently depreciate. While remote work and pandemic-induced migrations significantly impacted property desirability in previously marginal markets, the primary driver behind the surge in valuations was central bank monetary policies. Migration during the pandemic would have been much less if interest rates were 7% and quantitative easing (QE, where central banks create new money to buy bonds and lower borrowing costs) was not applied. Bitcoin fundamentally challenges this dynamic by providing a purely monetary asset with superior properties, ultimately aiming to remove this inflated monetary premium from real estate and returning the market to its genuine utility value.

Additionally, real estate transactions are slow and expensive, often taking months to finalize and burdened with steep costs and broker commissions that can easily reach 6–7% of the sale price.

Selling a $1 million property, for example, may leave the owner with $70,000 in expenses before they see their proceeds. By contrast, selling $1 million worth of bitcoin might cost only a few dollars in fees while settling almost instantly. Real estate also carries continuous costs, property taxes, insurance, and maintenance, whereas Bitcoin remains unencumbered, operating purely through mathematics and cryptographic security. But make no mistake, Bitcoin is property. It is an asset and it can be used as collateral.

The fusion of Bitcoin and real estate is already underway, reshaping traditional lending models. Bitcoin-backed lending enables investors to leverage their Bitcoin holdings without liquidating them, maintaining exposure to a superior asset while acquiring tangible property.

In a groundbreaking example, institutional investment adviser Newmarket Capital recently refinanced the Bank Street Court apartments in Old City, Philadelphia, using a loan collateralized by real estate and Bitcoin. The loan was secured by both the physical building and approximately 20 BTC.

As explained by Newmarket Capital CEO Andrew Hohns regarding their proactive Bitcoin-collateralized "Battery Finance" loans, "As lenders, we are constructive on the long-term value of Bitcoin and comfortable recognizing Bitcoin as collateral without mark-to-market risk … We have improved our downside through the introduction of Bitcoin, an uncorrelated element—an asset that has had such a strong appreciation over time—in the collateral package."[5]

This represents a fundamental shift. Borrowers no longer need to sell Bitcoin to access traditional assets; instead, they integrate Bitcoin into their broader investment strategies, using it as foundational collateral for debt. Such integration stabilizes property investments and enhances the resilience of borrowers' balance sheets by preserving their exposure to the hardest form of money ever created.

Some real estate investors are starting to fuse their properties with Bitcoin, integrating the network's superior financial engineering into their investment strategies. Firms such as Cardone Capital are already pioneering methods to effectively "back" real estate with Bitcoin. This fusion represents a critical inflection point, a dual compounding network effect.

On one side, capital exiting traditional real estate moves toward Bitcoin, boosting adoption and reinforcing Bitcoin's credibility as the superior store-of-value network. On the other side, those staying within or entering real estate recognize the necessity of integrating Bitcoin, thus further amplifying adoption. Real estate becomes increasingly Bitcoin-backed, creating a feedback loop that strengthens Bitcoin's position as a foundational economic infrastructure.

The recent wallet-to-wallet Bitcoin real estate transaction, a modest condo in Miami, sold directly for bitcoin,[6] captures this unprecedented shift vividly. Documented in my Substack article, "The Day Bitcoin Ate Real Estate,"[7] this milestone illustrates Bitcoin's expanding role as a trusted settlement layer for significant real-world assets. This transaction signaled a broader economic transition, reinforcing Bitcoin's inevitability as the monetary backbone of future asset markets.

While real estate remains essential, its limitations compared to Bitcoin are increasingly evident. Liquidity risks, taxation burdens, and government seizure persist in property ownership. Bitcoin, free from these barriers, operates independently without maintenance costs or operational risks, providing unmatched liquidity.

Furthermore, blockchain technology promises to eliminate inefficiencies in real estate transactions. Tokenized property ownership, built on Bitcoin's underlying principles, can enable fractional ownership, greater liquidity, and reduced transaction friction, streamlining a traditionally cumbersome industry.

We are witnessing a massive shift in how wealth is stored, transferred, and securitized. Capital traditionally flowing into real estate is starting to gravitate toward Bitcoin, a trend likely to accelerate, forcing property markets to adapt to a world where absolute mathematical scarcity, borderless transferability, and permissionless control reshape valuations permanently.

Real estate isn't disappearing; it's evolving. Bitcoin isn't replacing property, it's perfecting it.

Those recognizing this shift early will thrive. Those ignoring it will observe from the sidelines as history's most significant economic transformation unfolds.

CHAPTER 17

EGALITARIANISM

BITCOIN IS the most egalitarian monetary system ever conceived. It does not discriminate based on wealth, nationality, social status, or geography. It recognizes no borders and requires no permissions. Unlike traditional finance, where gatekeepers control access and privilege dictates opportunity, Bitcoin is equally accessible to everyone.

A farmer in Nigeria, a student in Argentina, a software developer in India, and a hedge fund manager in New York all interact with Bitcoin under identical conditions. There's no application process, no approval required, and no barriers to entry. If you have access to the internet, you have equal access to Bitcoin. A billionaire follows the same rules as a teenager. No bailouts, no money printing, no fractional reserve banking, no backroom deals. Bitcoin cannot be rigged in favor of insiders. Every transaction, every block, every wallet operates under the same mathematical principles.

Traditional finance, conversely, is a system built on exclusion. The wealthy and well-connected gain privileged access to capital, while everyone else faces inflation, fees, and limitations. Bitcoin removes these barriers through decentralization and governance solely by mathematics, code, and consensus. It remains unaffected by political climates and makes no exceptions for the powerful.

Bitcoin enforces fiscal discipline, unlike any monetary system before it. Bitcoin developer and cypherpunk "Uncle Rockstar Developer" perceptively explains:

We are at the level of complexity where states, especially big federal states in the US, it's not an efficient system, but it gets out of its own inefficiencies by printing more money instead of solving problems ... In the long run, Bitcoin will solve that inefficiency by enforcing fiscal discipline on states. You won't be able to print money to get out of the problems, you will need to recognize that you have failed. And once you recognize that you failed, that's the opportunity to try a different way or for someone else to step in, and governments can't do that.[1]

This insight reveals one of Bitcoin's most significant impacts: It mandates accountability.

Historically, governments presumed endless money printing could mask inefficiency and wastefulness. Rather than confronting errors, restructuring, or embracing innovation, they inflate currencies, indirectly taxing citizens and insulating insiders from consequences. Bitcoin removes this escape hatch.

Under a Bitcoin standard, governments lose the ability to obscure inefficiencies with inflation. They must address problems transparently, structurally, and honestly, without relying on monetary manipulation. Bitcoin not only grants financial sovereignty to individuals, it demands accountability from entire nations.

In the existing financial system, your money isn't truly yours. Your bank accounts can be frozen, assets seized, and savings devalued by inflation. A bureaucrat can deny your access to wealth. Bitcoin changes this entirely because it cannot be seized, inflated away, or manipulated by any government or institution.

For those living under oppressive regimes, the politically

targeted, or populations facing economic instability, Bitcoin represents genuine freedom.

Yet Bitcoin alone cannot erase all economic inequalities overnight. Wealth disparities remain. Those with greater initial resources naturally have easier entry into the system. Still, Bitcoin fundamentally changes the game. By removing discretion, manipulation, and corruption from money, it ensures everyone who participates does so under the same rules.

Bitcoin is the direct rejection of existing financial systems. Bitcoin declares: You don't need permission. The rules apply equally to everyone. Play fairly, and you win. For the first time, money belongs directly to individuals rather than institutions. Finally, a monetary system built on fairness rather than favoritism.

This is true egalitarian finance.

CHAPTER 18

BITCOIN AT SCALE

BITCOIN'S SCALABILITY has been one of its most hotly debated topics since inception. As adoption accelerates globally, so too does the demand for faster transactions, broader accessibility, and greater efficiency. Many critics have argued that Bitcoin cannot handle the scale required to operate as a global financial system, yet these concerns often misconstrue Bitcoin's fundamental nature and its inherent methods of scaling. In my opinion, Bitcoin's design and economic incentives position it to absorb enormous amounts of the world's capital. Once it reaches a valuation of $100 million per coin, one satoshi will equal one dollar—a clear demonstration of Bitcoin's unmatched capacity to scale economically.

At first glance, Bitcoin's scale invariance—monetary policy does not shift based on user growth— and its scalability may seem contradictory. Invariance means its rules never change. Unlike traditional financial systems, which require continuous manipulation of interest rates, liquidity injections, and monetary policy adjustments to accommodate economic growth and stability, Bitcoin's maximum supply remains fixed at 21 million coins. The block subsidy decreases predictably, and the protocol continues to function identically whether there are thousands or billions of users.

Bitcoin scales through multiple tiers, each serving specific functions. The base layer, the Bitcoin blockchain, is optimized for maximum security and settlement finality. It is not intended for small daily transactions like buying coffee. Instead, Bitcoin achieves true scalability through second-layer solutions, such as the Lightning Network and other innovative technologies built on top of the base layer.

The Lightning Network has emerged as Bitcoin's most successful scaling solution. It allows users to transact instantly, cheaply, and privately by processing payments off Bitcoin's main blockchain, known as "off-chain" transactions. Rather than recording every small payment directly on Bitcoin's base layer, Lightning uses secure, temporary payment channels between users. These channels rely on cryptographic contracts and digital signatures, ensuring transactions are authentic and preventing fraud. Lightning channels periodically settle their final balances back on Bitcoin's main blockchain, dramatically increasing Bitcoin's overall transaction capacity without compromising decentralization, security, or trustlessness.

Aside from the Lightning Network, other innovative technologies build upon Bitcoin's foundational security. For instance, sidechains are secondary blockchains that run parallel to the main Bitcoin blockchain, enabling specialized-use cases without burdening Bitcoin's primary network. Liquid, a prominent sidechain, allows institutions and traders to settle Bitcoin transactions faster and more privately. Another innovation, Rootstock, integrates Ethereum-like smart contract capabilities directly with Bitcoin, allowing for advanced decentralized financial (DeFi) services, the issuance of digital assets, and more complex transactions, all while maintaining Bitcoin's essential security and scarcity. These additional technologies allow Bitcoin to scale significantly, opening doors to DeFi, tokenization, and advanced financial applications without altering the fundamental qualities that make Bitcoin valuable.

Critics who claim Bitcoin cannot scale often overlook this layered approach. They mistake short-term base-layer congestion for permanent limitations. But Bitcoin is not simply another payment network, it is economic infrastructure designed to scale through innovation, layering, and network incentives.

This layered scaling approach ensures Bitcoin remains decentralized and secure, while simultaneously allowing it to become both a global reserve asset and a ubiquitous medium of exchange. Bitcoin scales differently because it must scale differently. It cannot compromise decentralization or trustlessness for speed or convenience.

It's no longer whether Bitcoin can scale.

It's who will be ready when it inevitably does.

CHAPTER 19

BITCOIN'S ECONOMIC IMPACT

BITCOIN IS INTRINSICALLY CHANGING how humans interact with money, value, and wealth. Far more than technological curiosity, it is an economic imperative reshaping global financial systems, altering asset allocation, redefining national sovereignty, and challenging deeply entrenched power structures. The world has reached a tipping point, transitioning irrevocably from skepticism and doubt to necessity and inevitability.

Bitcoin's adoption is occurring unevenly across the globe, driven by diverse motivations and operating on differing timelines. In economically stable nations, Bitcoin is primarily viewed as an inflation hedge, a superior store of value compared to traditional assets like gold, bonds, or real estate. Investors in these regions are gradually realizing that wealth kept as fiat currency will inevitably decay by inflation. Conversely, in countries plagued by currency devaluation and political instability, Bitcoin is a lifeline, a means of preserving wealth and economic sovereignty.

In Argentina, Nigeria, and El Salvador, Bitcoin is not a speculative asset; it's an economic necessity. Citizens use bitcoin daily, protecting their savings from hyperinflation and circumventing oppressive financial restrictions. In Argentina, citizens rely on bitcoin to preserve their life savings from rampant inflation and economic mismanagement. In Nigeria, where currency controls limit citizens' access to stable money, bitcoin has become a vital part of the informal economy. El Salvador took the unprecedented step of adopting bitcoin as legal tender, creating a national laboratory for economic freedom, financial inclusion, and sovereign independence. This bold experiment has led to increased financial access, improved international remittances, boosted tourism, and attracted investment in innovative infrastructure projects, showcasing Bitcoin's real-world impact on economic resilience and national independence.

Institutional adoption of Bitcoin further accelerates this economic transformation. Corporations such as Strategy, Square, Metaplanet, Semler Scientific, GameStop, and Tesla have placed Bitcoin on their balance sheets. Financial institutions, including giants like BlackRock and Fidelity, have integrated Bitcoin through ETFs, legitimizing Bitcoin for traditional investors worldwide. This institutionalization brings stability, liquidity, and maturity to the market, facilitating further adoption by businesses, pension funds, sovereign wealth funds, and nation-states.

Bitcoin propels nations toward genuine economic reform. Sovereign adoption of Bitcoin as a reserve asset will become inevitable, reshaping international power dynamics and accelerating global economic realignment. This new economic reality also facilitates unprecedented global financial inclusion. Billions remain unbanked, excluded from the traditional financial system, deprived of basic banking and investment opportunities. Bitcoin's decentralized, permissionless nature grants universal access to secure savings, instant global transfers, and economic participation. The Lightning Network further enhances this, enabling instantaneous micropayments and making decentralized financial services accessible even to those living without traditional banking infrastructure.

A generational shift is underway, marking the largest wealth transfer in human history. Baby Boomers, holding significant wealth in traditional asset classes, are passing it to Millennials and Gen Z, both native to the digital world and more intuitively aligned with Bitcoin's promising future. Younger generations will not lose their purchasing power by parking inherited wealth in bonds or in overpriced real estate burdened with taxes and maintenance costs. They will gravitate toward Bitcoin, embracing its simplicity, accessibility, and absolute scarcity. And if you're Gen X like me, you're probably just feeling lucky to be here.

In this new economic paradigm, there is no middle ground. The shift toward Bitcoin is already happening as it steadily reshapes the economic landscape beneath our feet.

The choice for individuals, corporations, and nations is now clear:

Adapt to Bitcoin or be left behind.

CHAPTER 20

BANKS AND UNBANKING

TRADITIONAL BANKS HAVE ALWAYS SAT at the center of money, controlling who can access financial services, who qualifies for loans, what fees are charged, and the extent to which inflation steadily weakens purchasing power. For centuries, they dictated the terms, standing as intermediaries between you and your money. But Bitcoin changes everything.

For the first time, people are not merely moving money from one bank to another; they are moving capital entirely out of the fiat system. This isn't a temporary trend. It's a one-way door. Banks are witnessing this in real-time.

Imagine working in the risk department of a major financial institution, monitoring daily transaction flows. Every day, thousands of small withdrawals leave checking accounts, heading directly to Bitcoin exchanges. The patterns are clear: recurring buys of $100 every Tuesday at lunch, $500 each payday, or lump-sum transfers during market dips. It's not just retail investors. Professionals, business owners, and high-net-worth individuals are also moving their wealth out of the traditional financial system.

At first, banks dismissed these shifts. Perhaps they assumed

Bitcoin was just another overhyped bubble, comparable to the dot-com era or the subprime mortgage frenzy. But this money didn't return. It wasn't reinvested into equities or parked temporarily in savings accounts—it permanently exited the fiat ecosystem.

This trend represents so much more than crypto trading or speculative gambling on altcoins; this is an exit strategy.

At some point, banking executives must ask themselves: How can we prevent this? Should we integrate Bitcoin services? Are we losing these customers permanently? The uncomfortable truth is brutal. They can't stop Bitcoin, they can't outcompete it; instead, they're losing capital forever.

Even if banks attempt to incorporate Bitcoin into their offerings, they're competing against a system that doesn't need them. Bitcoin requires no loans, permissions, or intermediaries. It offers self-sovereign finance, and once wealth is stored in Bitcoin, reliance on banks fades.

Most underestimate how scarce Bitcoin truly is. There are 8 billion people in the world, only 21 million Bitcoin, and the majority of the remaining coins are tightly held by long-term holders, institutional investors, and sovereign wealth funds, groups who have recognized Bitcoin's value early or made significant investments based on market-driven choices. Retail investors continue steadily accumulating wealth through strategies like dollar-cost averaging and rarely selling. Worldwide exchange reserves shrunk from roughly 3.1 million BTC in July 2024 to about 2.8 million BTC (about 14.5% of circulating supply) in early July 2025, the lowest level since 2018,[1] and each halving further diminishes new supply issuance. Importantly, unlike traditional financial systems, Bitcoin's distribution isn't structurally privileged or artificially maintained. It reflects organic adoption and open market participation, accessible to anyone.

Banks see these statistics. They monitor the capital outflows daily and increasingly recognize the permanence of this migration. These outflows signify a structural change in global finance.

The traditional banking system rests on three pillars: trust, debt, and inflation. Customers must trust banks to secure their money, continue borrowing to sustain debt-driven growth, and accept ongoing inflation to service this growing debt. Bitcoin undermines all three pillars simultaneously. It removes trust from the equation through self-custody; reduces reliance on debt because Bitcoin is a pristine asset, not someone else's liability; and defies inflation with an immutable, fixed supply.

Banks will undoubtedly resist. They will attempt to regulate Bitcoin, impose restrictions, introduce central bank digital currencies (CBDCs), and delay the inevitable transition. But they cannot stop individuals from opting out.

The world is waking up. Fiat currency is deteriorating. Bitcoin is where capital is flowing, and there's no going back.

CHAPTER 21

THE PATH TO MAXIMALISM

MY WIFE USED to tell me I wasn't allowed to talk about Bitcoin when we went out to dinner. I became like the friend I mentioned in the introduction, passionately preaching about Bitcoin in 2012. Back then, I thought he was annoying. Now, I realize he was ahead of his time, and I'm the one who can't stop talking about Bitcoin. I'm the one who sees it everywhere, in everything. Once Bitcoin enters your mind, it never leaves. It's an infection with no cure. But why would I want a cure? To return to a system I now recognize as broken? There's no unseeing what I've seen. There is no going back. Within the Bitcoin community, we call this awakening "taking the orange pill," a reference to the movie *The Matrix*, symbolizing a choice to see the financial system as it truly is. Bitcoin is the orange pill that, once taken, shatters the illusions of the existing monetary world, providing a clear path to genuine financial freedom outside "the matrix" of traditional finance.

At first the frustration was intense. No one wanted to listen, to learn, or even to discuss Bitcoin seriously. Conversations were met with polite nods, uncomfortable laughter, or sharp comments that "it's not real money." It was isolating, until I realized that this isolation was guiding me toward something deeper. With no one to discuss my insights with, the energy became so intense it had to manifest somewhere. It compelled me to write. And from that urgency, this book was born.

The transformation happens subtly but profoundly. Many years ago, in the late 1990s, I attended The Barbara Brennan School of Healing. Central to this experience was "The Healer's Journey," mirroring the Hero's Journey—a descent into profound transformation, emerging with a gift to share. At the time, I couldn't imagine how those spiritual insights would intertwine with my financial journey, but they did. Discovering Bitcoin was my personal "Healer's Journey," pulling me deep into economics, cryptography, and philosophy—reshaping my very identity.

I started as simply curious, then became a trader, then an investor. Eventually, I found myself passionately advocating for Bitcoin. But even that wasn't the end; a deeper truth awaited. Gradually, almost imperceptibly, I became a maximalist—a firm believer that Bitcoin is the only true monetary asset of lasting value. Maximalism isn't a choice; it's recognition of an undeniable truth. My perspective shifted permanently; I stopped measuring wealth in dollars and started measuring it only in Bitcoin.

This wasn't just economic, it was philosophical and spiritual. Just as my spiritual development taught me to see hidden forces shaping reality, Bitcoin revealed hidden truths about money, power, and autonomy.

Bitcoin recalibrates your thinking, shifting your focus from immediate gratification to long-term decision-making, anchored not in short-term cycles or quarterly outcomes but in a deeper understanding of economics and value preservation embedded within its design. Fiat currency becomes obviously irrational, its inflation and manipulation unsustainable. Selling bitcoin back into fiat feels reckless, like trading truth for illusion, autonomy for dependency, freedom for captivity.

Discovering Bitcoin was earth-shattering. It freed my mind from the fog of a failed financial system, a relentless, anxiety-inducing treadmill. As I studied Bitcoin, my inner discipline strengthened. I realized a lot of my anxiety stemmed from financial insecurity and mistrust in my future, causing painful waiting. Yet when I trusted—truly trusted—I felt energized, propelled forward confidently. Absolute trust seems impossibly difficult until you find it. And Bitcoin embodies trust precisely because it requires no trust, no intermediaries, no flawed human promises, only unbreakable math and undeniable truth.

Maximalists recognize Bitcoin as not merely the best money, but the only logical monetary system. Money is a winner-takes-all game, and Bitcoin has already won.

Maximalists don't trade Bitcoin because nothing is superior to it. Bitcoin is something we "hold on for dear life" (HODL); it's something we protect. More than a financial stance, it's a moral imperative, a commitment to responsibility, discipline, and a rejection of corrupt fiat systems. Bitcoin is the power to liberate yourself from a broken economic system. This freedom isn't theoretical; it's tangible and powerful.

Maximalism is transformation and the inevitable recognition of Bitcoin's absolute superiority. Bitcoin is not just money; it's a new economic truth. Bitcoin maximalism isn't something you choose.

It's something you become.

CHAPTER 22

MICHAEL SAYLOR'S EPIPHANY

MICHAEL SAYLOR, founder and executive chairman of Strategy, formerly MicroStrategy (MSTR), wasn't early to embrace Bitcoin. For years, he dismissed it, even tweeting skeptically about its potential in 2013. Like many successful corporate leaders entrenched in traditional finance, Saylor initially overlooked Bitcoin, focusing instead on conventional methods of preserving and growing wealth. But when clarity arrived, it hit him with unstoppable force.

In 2020, Saylor experienced what many now call his Bitcoin awakening. As CEO of MicroStrategy, a publicly traded software firm, he had amassed a significant cash reserve intended as a hedge against financial uncertainty. But upon deeper reflection, Saylor realized something critical: Cash was no longer a safe asset. It was losing purchasing power rapidly due to central banks' continual printing of money.

"For the first time in the history of the human race, we're able to store and channel monetary energy without power loss."[1]

This realization changed everything for MicroStrategy, and for Saylor personally. He recognized that traditional stores of wealth, such as cash, bonds, stocks, and even gold, were fundamentally flawed. They all carried counterparty risk, could be diluted, inflated away, or confiscated. Bitcoin, he discovered, was different. It wasn't just an asset; it was an incorruptible store of monetary energy, perfectly engineered and mathematically enforced.

In August 2020, Michael Saylor made a historic move by allocating $250 million of MicroStrategy's cash reserves, when Bitcoin was trading around $11,000 per coin, to acquire 21,454 BTC.[2] At the time, MicroStrategy held roughly $500–$600 million in cash, so this initial plunge represented about half of its liquid assets.[3] Many in the financial world considered it reckless and heavily criticized the decision. Yet Saylor recognized a key insight, "Bitcoin is money. Everything else is credit."[4]

This decision was not impulsive; it was strategic. Soon after the initial purchase, MicroStrategy escalated its commitment, accumulating more Bitcoin through corporate bonds and equity offerings. By July 2025, the company held nearly 630,000 bitcoin,[5] making it the largest corporate bitcoin holder in the world.

Saylor's conviction was absolute. He famously declared: "I'll be buying at the top forever."[6]

Strategy was no longer purely a software company; it had become a de facto Bitcoin holding company, with its stock widely considered a proxy for institutional Bitcoin exposure.

THE INSTITUTIONAL DOMINO EFFECT

Strategy's entry into Bitcoin sent shockwaves through the corporate and financial worlds. Following Saylor's lead, corporations such as Tesla, Block (formerly Square), and others began adding Bitcoin to their balance sheets. Financial giants like Fidelity and BlackRock rapidly moved to offer Bitcoin ETFs, custody services, and structured products, further legitimizing Bitcoin as a mainstream institutional asset.

Saylor openly admits he wasn't early to Bitcoin, but he was

early enough to change the narrative. His clear, unapologetic articulation of Bitcoin's value proposition reshaped Wall Street's view. Institutions that once scoffed at Bitcoin now scrambled to integrate it into their portfolios.

A NEW CORPORATE STRATEGY

Before Bitcoin, corporate treasury management revolved around traditional, often ineffective strategies:

- Holding cash or bonds, vulnerable to inflation.
- Buying back stock to artificially inflate share prices.
- Making questionable acquisitions, driven more by optics than strategic value.

Strategy shattered these norms. Its treasury became a fortress built entirely upon Bitcoin's financial strength. The company was no longer exposed to inflation or currency debasement. It had exited the fiat system entirely, pioneering a new corporate financial paradigm. Strategy's balance sheet transformed into a proxy for the hardest asset on earth, its stock serving as a vehicle for institutions seeking indirect Bitcoin exposure. And Strategy is no longer alone. Today, this corporate embrace of Bitcoin is accelerating at a remarkable pace. At the start of 2025, about sixty publicly traded companies reported holding Bitcoin on their balance sheets. By August of the same year, that number had surged past 160[7]—more than doubling in just a few months. This rapid growth underscores how quickly Bitcoin is moving from the margins to the center of corporate finance, validating Saylor's bold conviction and signaling what may become the dominant corporate strategy of the digital age.

A VISIONARY FINANCING PLAYBOOK: CONVERTIBLES, AN ATM, AND PREFERRED SHARES

What makes Strategy's approach so remarkable isn't simply its decision to hold Bitcoin, but how it raised capital to acquire it. Under Michael Saylor's direction, the company built a financing playbook in phases, moving from convertible debt, to an at-the-market equity program, and most recently, to perpetual preferred stock.

Phase 1: Convertible Senior Notes (2020–2023)

At the outset, Strategy issued a series of convertible senior notes —low-interest debt instruments that can later convert into shares— such as the 0.75% notes due in 2025, the 0% notes due in 2027, the 0.625% notes due in 2030, 2.25% due in 2032, and the 0% notes due in 2030.[8] These were sold privately to institutional buyers under Rule 144A and provided billions in initial capital that seeded the company's Bitcoin accumulation.

Phase 2: At-the-Market (ATM) Equity Program (Aug 2023–present)

Once its balance sheet was recognized as a Bitcoin proxy, Strategy launched an ATM program, gradually issuing new MSTR shares directly into the market.[9] Normally, issuing new stock dilutes existing shareholders. But Saylor argued that because ATM proceeds were immediately converted into Bitcoin, the company's per-share economic exposure to Bitcoin could still rise—a dynamic he called "accretive dilution."

Phase 3: Perpetual Preferreds (2025–present)

Most recently, Strategy added a suite of perpetual preferred shares with annual dividends ranging from 8% to 10%, including STRC (increased from 9% to 10% in September 2025), STRD (10%), STRF (10%), and STRK (8%).[10] These preferreds opened another channel for institutional capital to flow into Bitcoin exposure through a trusted corporate vehicle, further cementing Strategy's role as a financial innovator.

Together, these instruments transformed Strategy from a traditional software firm into a leveraged Bitcoin holding company. Its financing innovations provided a template that other corporations may study as they consider integrating Bitcoin into their own treasuries.

THE FUTURE OF STRATEGY

Strategy is integrating Bitcoin deeply into its financial DNA by:

- Using Bitcoin as collateral in corporate borrowing.
- Building internal custody/controls for a large corporate BTC treasury and sharing that playbook publicly.
- Serving as a corporate Bitcoin investment vehicle, effectively acting as a leveraged Bitcoin ETF proxy.

Michael Saylor, once a skeptic, became its most vocal institutional advocate through conviction born of deep understanding.

In August 2020, before Strategy adopted Bitcoin, the company's market capitalization stood around $1.4 billion.[11] Just five years later, after strategically accumulating nearly 630,000 bitcoin, Strategy's market capitalization soared dramatically, surpassing $113.95 billion by July of 2025.[12] This extraordinary growth directly demonstrates a profound validation of Saylor's bold, Bitcoin-focused corporate blueprint.

I've learned immensely from listening to Saylor's insights and hold deep admiration for his clarity and conviction. For anyone eager to truly comprehend Bitcoin's significance, I highly recommend exploring Michael Saylor's interviews and presentations on YouTube—his perspective is invaluable.

"I think that Bitcoin is an enlightened and peaceful way to settle our differences on a global basis. I think that, in a way, it demonetizes the incentives for war."[13] – Michael Saylor

Saylor didn't create Bitcoin, nor was he early. But once he understood its power, he committed completely, influencing countless others to see Bitcoin's true potential and changing the financial landscape permanently.

CHAPTER 23

CREATIVITY AND TIME

BITCOIN UNLOCKS something far deeper than financial security. It liberates time.

Most people don't realize it yet, but Bitcoin offers a way out of the perpetual economic trap created by fiat currency. It frees people from the endless cycle of trading their time for a depreciating currency. Under the fiat system, people must work harder every year just to make ends meet, constantly trying to outpace inflation, rising costs, and mounting debt. Work, for many, is not a choice but a necessity of survival—a perpetual human hamster wheel.

Bitcoin disrupts this cycle.

By preserving and appreciating economic energy over time, Bitcoin empowers people to store the value of their labor without erosion. Bitcoin provides the tools to get ahead, to afford more time for creativity, personal interests, and planning for the future. This is called lowering your time preference. It works because everything gets less expensive over time when priced in Bitcoin (see Figure 15).

Over time things cost less when priced in Bitcoin

Year		Price (USD)	Price (BTC)
2017	🏠	$384,900	96 ₿
2021	🏠	$464,200	9.7 ₿
2025	🏠	$526,993	4.71 ₿

Figure 15: The Changing Value of Real Estate When
Priced in Bitcoin

Fiat money traps humanity in short-term thinking, high-time preference, fight or flight mode. People chase immediate gratification because saving in fiat is futile; you trade your life energy for money that dwindles before you can fully utilize it.

With Bitcoin, long-term planning becomes rational and meaningful. Saving ceases to be a gamble; it's a guaranteed way to preserve purchasing power. The discipline of accumulation teaches patience, fosters creativity, and opens doors to possibilities previously unimaginable. When wealth no longer melts away, people gain the room to breathe, dream, and create.

Consider the countless potential geniuses trapped in jobs they despise, forced to focus their energy solely on basic survival instead of innovation or creative expression. How many brilliant minds never get the chance to pursue their passions because they're overwhelmed by financial pressures?

Bitcoin lifts this weight.

This isn't solely about investing; it's about reclaiming the most precious resource we have: time. Time to think, innovate, and contribute something meaningful to the world. How many of us have said, "I'd love to pursue this or that, but I don't have the time or money"? When you choose to store your economic energy in

Bitcoin, your money works for you over time. The result is financial breathing room, allowing you to pursue dreams and interests that seemed forever out of reach.

As an artist and someone who was stuck in the endless maze of the fiat system for nearly fifty years, Bitcoin has been a gift unlike any other. I increasingly have more time to pursue what truly matters to me.

As Bitcoin adoption grows, each fractional bitcoin, each satoshi, becomes increasingly precious. In the future, whole bitcoins will be unimaginable luxuries. Future generations will marvel:

"Imagine if we had the chance to buy just one bitcoin back then."

Yet even now, most people ignore the opportunity before them, unaware that this window is closing. Those recognizing this shift today have an opportunity future generations will envy. Someday soon, people will look back and say, "If only we had understood Bitcoin sooner."

With Bitcoin you stop living moment-to-moment, paycheck-to-paycheck, and start thinking in decades and generations. Bitcoin frees people to think, create, and build. It's more than just an investment; it's a shift in human consciousness.

Bitcoin liberates creativity.

Bitcoin returns your time to its rightful owner.

CHAPTER 24

GLOBAL IMPACT

BITCOIN IS NOT A ONCE-IN-A-GENERATION EVENT, it is a *once-in-a-civilization event*. We are fortunate to be alive at the beginning of the opportunity to escape the broken fiat economy. Today, Bitcoin is rapidly becoming the cornerstone of a new global economic order. Governments, institutions, and global financial systems are all being forced to react, not because they want to, but because they must.

From the earliest days of civilization, financial systems have been instruments of control, wielded by empires, governments, and central banks to dictate the rules of economic engagement. Currency debasement, inflation, and monetary policy manipulation have always existed. Bitcoin ends this era definitively by permanently separating money from state control.

BITCOIN'S GLOBAL ADOPTION: A POLITICAL REVOLUTION

When El Salvador declared bitcoin legal tender in 2021, the decision was mocked by the global financial elite. But what began as a single nation's bold experiment soon became a worldwide phenomenon.

In countries where fiat currency has already failed, Bitcoin is a lifeline:

- **Argentina**, crippled by inflation exceeding 200% annually, is quietly embracing Bitcoin as an alternative to the collapsing peso.
- **Turkey**, struggling with a rapidly depreciating currency, the lira, has seen explosive growth in Bitcoin adoption as citizens seek a secure alternative immune to debasement.
- In Africa, **Nigeria** has become one of the fastest-growing Bitcoin markets. Everyday citizens use Bitcoin to circumvent oppressive monetary controls and exorbitant remittance fees. Remarkably, Nigeria is even integrating Bitcoin education into grammar-school curriculums, actively preparing future generations for financial empowerment.
- **Hong Kong** has embraced Bitcoin to reposition itself as a global financial hub, despite China's continued hostile stance toward cryptocurrencies.
- **Bhutan**, seeking economic resilience, has significantly engaged in state-backed Bitcoin mining initiatives, leveraging the country's abundant hydropower resources to strengthen national self-sufficiency and diversify its economic foundations.

Governments resisting Bitcoin face a losing battle. China banned mining, only to see mining operations quickly relocate else-where, stronger than ever. The European Union attempts tighter regulation yet implicitly acknowledges Bitcoin's resilience by shifting regulatory focus from outright restrictions toward clearer frameworks for its safe integration, recognizing the asset's growing permanence in global finance. In the United States, Bitcoin has become increasingly politicized, embraced by some as a pathway to economic freedom and opposed by others who fear losing monetary control. Despite reluctance, the momentum is irreversible. Bitcoin adoption will continue to accelerate because it solves problems fiat systems create: inflation, financial censorship, and centralized manipulation.

Bitcoin doesn't care about political parties, religious affiliations, or personal beliefs—it exists outside of these divisions (see Figure 16). Bitcoin isn't aligned with people; rather, people become aligned with Bitcoin. As individuals awaken to its significance and impartiality, they naturally affiliate with its ideals, not the other way around.

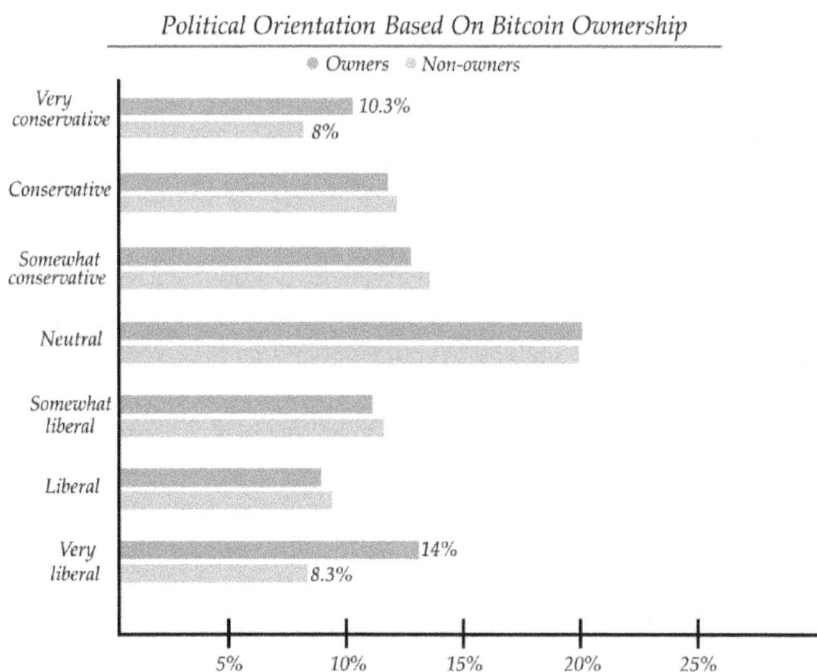

Political Orientation Based On Bitcoin Ownership

● Owners   ● Non-owners

Very conservative — 10.3% / 8%

Conservative

Somewhat conservative

Neutral

Somewhat liberal

Liberal

Very liberal — 14% / 8.3%

5%   10%   15%   20%   25%

Figure 16: Political Orientation Based on Bitcoin Ownership

Bitcoin's Monetary Infrastructure Revolution

Bitcoin's integration into global finance is absorbing, streamlining, and replacing outdated financial infrastructure.

- Bitcoin-backed lending and collateralization are reshaping how capital flows. Instead of pledging cumbersome real estate or devaluing fiat currency, Bitcoin holders can borrow against a mathematically verifiable asset with no counterparty risk.
- Tokenization of traditional assets, including real estate, will move on-chain, eliminating inefficiencies, improving liquidity, and democratizing investment opportunities.
- Bitcoin-based remittances are revolutionizing cross-border payments, providing instantaneous transfers at minimal costs, removing intermediaries, and enhancing global financial inclusion.

These innovations redefine the rules entirely.

Mining, Energy, and National Security

The global struggle for hash rate dominance is becoming a significant geopolitical battleground. Nations increasingly realize that securing Bitcoin mining capacity is equivalent to acquiring strategic digital real estate, territory that will define future economic power.

Countries like the United States, Russia, and various Middle Eastern nations now recognize mining centers as essential infrastructure and are investing heavily in mining operations to secure their place in Bitcoin's emerging economic order.

Bitcoin as the Global Reserve Asset

Central banks and sovereign wealth funds are beginning to integrate Bitcoin into their reserves. As more nations adopt Bitcoin, those who fail to participate risk being left behind, economically isolated in a rapidly changing world order.

Fiat currencies historically survive around thirty to forty years before collapsing under inflation.[1] Examples include the German papiermark (hyperinflation culminating in 1923), the Hungarian pengő (collapse in 1946), Zimbabwe (2007–2008 hyperinflation), and, more recently, Venezuela (entered hyperinflation in late 2016).[2] Bitcoin, designed for multigenerational longevity, stands in stark contrast to these failures. It isn't simply another asset to be regulated, it is a direct challenge to central banking itself. My belief is that, at some point, the dollar will be backed by Bitcoin.

The world has already changed; most just haven't realized it yet.

CHAPTER 25

BITCOIN, WAR, AND THE
BATTLE FOR HASH POWER

THROUGHOUT HISTORY, wars have revolved around the command of resources. Empires have risen and fallen over land, oil, gold, and trade routes. The nation that controlled critical resources held power and dominance. But the landscape is shifting, and the wars of tomorrow won't be fought solely on physical battlegrounds; they will be fought digitally, economically, and energetically. Bitcoin sits at this new paradigm's core, actively shaping and driving geopolitical, economic, and strategic realignment globally.

US Space Force Guardian Major Jason P. Lowery's influential book *Softwar*[1] provides a powerful vision of how geopolitical conflict is evolving from traditional forms of warfare to one in which computational dominance is paramount. Lowery recognized something extraordinary: Bitcoin mining represents the digitization of war itself as an evolution from kinetic violence to energy-based security. While individual nation-states may attempt to gain strategic advantage by controlling significant portions of the Bitcoin network's hash rate, Bitcoin's decentralized and globally distributed nature makes absolute dominance or permanent control practically impossible. Rather than facilitating centralized control, this competitive dynamic incentivizes nations to continuously invest in computational infrastructure, collectively strengthening Bitcoin's security and resilience.

In January 2025, advocates proposed that the United States establish a national Strategic Bitcoin Reserve—an idea that, if implemented, would mark a profound shift in how nations approach monetary and energy policy. What began with a humble white paper published anonymously in 2008 has now become a strategic asset under serious discussion at the highest levels of government. Bitcoin has transitioned from an obscure digital curiosity into an indispensable component of national security.

Today, computational power and energy are becoming critical strategic assets because they underpin the security and control of economic sovereignty in the digital age. Money is no longer locked in vaults; it's stored permanently in cyberspace within the most powerful computer network in the world. Bitcoin mining, which transforms real-world electricity into digital monetary security, has emerged as a new frontier of geopolitical competition. Nations increasingly realize that securing hash power—computational dominance—is now strategically comparable to controlling vital resources like oil fields or critical trade routes.

Bitcoin is a national-security technology. Proof of Work turns energy and computational power into a defense system that anyone can verify, and nations will compete for it. Countries that anchor significant hash rate (the aggregate computing power securing the network) gain strategic leverage: They harden their savings base, cultivate flexible industrial demand for energy, and keep a meaningful share of the network's security budget onshore. The United States already leads with about 37.8% of global hash rate by geolocated pool data as of January 2022; and in 2025, a Cambridge survey of mining operators (representing about 48% of the network's total hash rate) found that 75.4% of that reported activity was located in the United States.[2] The methodology is different from the earlier geolocation data, but both point to the same conclusion: America is out in front, and there is an active race to build domestic mining capacity.

Countries facing international sanctions, such as Russia and Iran, view Bitcoin as a potential means to maintain economic autonomy, bypass restrictions, and facilitate trade. Meanwhile, nations like El Salvador embrace Bitcoin openly and transparently to ensure financial independence, innovation, and economic inclusion. Bitcoin itself remains neutral—accessible equally to all countries—highlighting its capacity both to empower innovation and to challenge traditional geopolitical structures. Bitcoin undermines traditional methods of economic warfare, sanctions, asset seizures, and capital controls. This changes the strategic calculus. Financial statecraft becomes more complex, more subtle, and far more contested.

Sanctions lose much of their effectiveness when nations transact in bitcoin. Economic trade routes become digital, invisible, and impossible to blockade financially. While Bitcoin cannot remove physical blockades that prevent goods and aid from reaching populations, it fundamentally transforms how monetary value itself moves in a world where wealth can be transferred instantly, securely, and without reliance on traditional intermediaries. When we say it separates money and state, it's not just the United States—it's the entire planet.

The transition toward a Bitcoin-centric financial order has already begun, and it is accelerating. Nations that fail to see this new reality will quickly find themselves economically irrelevant in a digital age. Those who lead in Bitcoin mining will secure their economic futures, stabilize their energy grids, and gain significant geopolitical leverage.

Bitcoin isn't just rewriting the rules of money.

It's rewriting the rules of war.

CHAPTER 26

THE FUTURE OF BITCOIN

THE WORLD IS FUNDAMENTALLY different now. Bitcoin is going far beyond reshaping finance; it's transforming our relationship with energy, economics, society, and even ourselves. Yet we are only sixteen years into this Bitcoin era. Pause and reflect on that—just sixteen short years into something that might very well last longer than anything humanity has ever built.

Today, we write books, produce podcasts, and confidently discuss Bitcoin's impact. We debate cycles, halvings, power laws, and network effects as if we've fully grasped this phenomenon. But the truth is, we have barely scratched the surface. Imagine what it will accomplish in one hundred or one thousand years. When future generations look back, will they marvel at our foresight, or smile at how little we truly understood?

We speak of four-year cycles as immutable laws of nature, yet we may soon discover even longer epochs like forty-year cycles, four-hundred-year cycles, or perhaps something special emerging uniquely every four halvings. Bitcoin might be even more transformative on a scale we have barely begun to comprehend.

Moreover, the true potential of Bitcoin emerges when you move from theoretical understanding to practical experience because learning about Bitcoin can only take you so far. Real empowerment is unlocked when you actively engage in buying bitcoin, managing your own private keys, consolidating UTXOs, updating wallet firmware, running your own miner, and perhaps even setting up a full node. These practical steps transform knowledge into true self-sovereignty.

I'm not naturally inclined toward technology, and learning something new often feels uncomfortable. Yet Bitcoin pushed me into that discomfort, and through it I experienced profound growth. With each step I built genuine confidence, clarity, and discipline. Bitcoin offers a form of economic self-defense against the uncertainties of our modern world.

We now stand at a critical crossroads, facing two potential futures:

One future is centralized, regulated, controlled by governments and corporations—a world dominated by central bank digital currencies (CBDCs) that monitor every transaction, enforce taxation, and dictate economic actions.

The other future is decentralized, sovereign, open source, and liberated. A future defined by permissionless innovation, individual sovereignty, and transparent economic power. We are already witnessing which future is emerging.

All we can do today is describe what we've observed in these first embryonic years. The true story, deeper revelations, and profound shifts have yet to fully unfold.

Thank you for joining me on this exploration. I am grateful to you, the reader, for sharing in this journey. If this book has opened your eyes, sparked your curiosity, or ignited your path of discovery, it has fulfilled its purpose. My hope is that you continue your quest beyond theory, from curiosity to mastery, from intellectual understanding to personal empowerment.

I look forward to continuing this adventure with you in Volume II.

Glossary

Adoption Curve: A model illustrating the rate at which new technologies or innovations are embraced by the public. Typically divided into stages: Innovators, Early Adopters, Early Majority, Late Majority, and Laggards. Bitcoin is currently transitioning from the Early Adopters stage to the Early Majority stage as global adoption accelerates.

Altcoin: Any cryptocurrency that is not Bitcoin. Altcoins often attempt to improve upon Bitcoin's original protocol, offering features such as different consensus mechanisms or increased transaction capabilities. However, they drastically fail to achieve Bitcoin's decentralized security and true scarcity.

Anonymous: A condition of complete identity concealment. Bitcoin transactions are often mistakenly described as anonymous; however, they are actually pseudonymous—transactions are publicly visible on the blockchain but linked only to public addresses, not personal identities.

Antifragile: A concept popularized by Nassim Nicholas Taleb to describe systems that strengthen and improve when exposed to volatility, shocks, or other stressors. Bitcoin exemplifies antifragility, as it consistently becomes stronger and more secure with each attack, challenge, or criticism it faces.

Application-Specific Integrated Circuit (ASIC): Specialized computer hardware engineered explicitly for mining cryptocurrencies, notably Bitcoin. ASIC miners perform the SHA-256 algorithm with exceptional efficiency, significantly increasing hash rate and improving network security.

Asset: Any resource or property owned that holds economic value, typically convertible to cash. Bitcoin has emerged as a premier digital asset due to its absolute scarcity, global liquidity, and incorruptibility.

Bailout: An act of government or central banks providing financial assistance to banks or corporations to prevent collapse. Bitcoin emerged during the 2008 financial crisis as a direct response to this practice, offering an alternative system immune to such interventions.

Bit: The basic unit of digital information, represented as either 0 or 1. Also commonly used informally to refer to a fractional amount of Bitcoin.

Bitcoin: The first decentralized digital currency, created by Satoshi Nakamoto in 2008. Bitcoin operates on a peer-to-peer network without intermediaries, governed purely by mathematics, cryptography, and consensus, ensuring scarcity, transparency, and resistance to censorship or manipulation.

Bitcoin-Backed Lending: A financial service that allows Bitcoin holders to borrow cash or stablecoins by using their Bitcoin as collateral. Instead of selling their Bitcoin, borrowers lock it with a lender and receive a loan, typically at a lower interest rate than unsecured credit. This lets them access liquidity while maintaining long-term Bitcoin exposure.

Bitcoin Core: The primary, open-source software that Bitcoin is implemented on, maintained by a global community of developers. Bitcoin Core validates transactions, secures the blockchain, and enables full nodes to enforce consensus rules. It is the Bitcoin network's software infrastructure.

Bitcoin Dominance: The metric measuring Bitcoin's market capitalization relative to the total cryptocurrency market. Higher Bitcoin dominance correlates to increased confidence and lower speculative risk.

Bitcoin Maximalist: Someone who believes Bitcoin is the only true digital asset of lasting value, viewing all altcoins strictly as cryptocurrencies that are considered inferior, unnecessary, or harmful distractions. Maximalists prioritize Bitcoin's decentralized integrity, security, absolute scarcity, and sound monetary principles, firmly distinguishing Bitcoin as the sole genuine digital asset within a vast sea of cryptocurrencies.

Bitcoiner: An individual who deeply understands, supports, and actively engages with Bitcoin, often advocating for its widespread adoption.

Block: A collection of grouped transactions, validated by miners and added to the blockchain. Each block contains a cryptographic reference (hash) linking it securely to the previous block, chaining together historical records.

Block Height: The total number of blocks that have been mined since the genesis block (the first block mined by Satoshi Nakamoto). Block height acts as a precise chronological marker for transactions within the blockchain.

Block Reward/Block Subsidy: The amount of Bitcoin awarded to a miner for successfully mining a new block. Initially set at 50 BTC, the reward is halved approximately every four years (every 210,000 blocks), a process known as "the Halving."

Block Size: The maximum data capacity of a single block in the blockchain. Bitcoin blocks were originally limited to 1 megabyte, designed to preserve decentralization by enabling easier node participation. Debate over block size has influenced Bitcoin's scalability solutions.

Block Time: The average interval between the creation of new blocks. For Bitcoin, the block time is approximately ten minutes, regulated by the Difficulty Adjustment, which maintains consistent issuance and security.

Blockchain: A decentralized, distributed digital ledger recording all Bitcoin transactions chronologically and immutably. Each block cryptographically secures the previous one, creating an unchangeable historical record maintained by a global network of nodes.

Blockchain Fork: An event where a blockchain splits into two separate chains due to disagreement among nodes or developers based on the network's rules or protocol. Forks can be temporary or permanent, resulting in separate cryptocurrencies (e.g., Bitcoin and Bitcoin Cash).

Bollinger Bands: A technical analysis indicator developed by John Bollinger, consisting of a centerline (simple moving average) and two bands above and below, measuring market volatility. Used to identify potential price breakouts, reversals, and trading opportunities in Bitcoin's price charts.

BTC: The widely accepted ticker symbol for Bitcoin, used on exchanges and financial platforms worldwide. Also frequently used informally to refer to a single Bitcoin.

Burn/Burned: The process of permanently removing Bitcoin from circulation by sending it to an irretrievable address, typically done intentionally to reduce supply, demonstrate scarcity, or symbolize commitment. Bitcoin may also be unintentionally removed from circulation through accidental loss. In either case, burning effectively reduces the circulating supply.

Candlesticks: Graphical representations of price movements, showing open, high, low, and close prices over specific intervals. Candlestick patterns help traders interpret market psychology, momentum, and potential reversals in Bitcoin's price.

Cantillon Effect: The economic phenomenon where newly created money disproportionately benefits those closest to its creation, disadvantaging others by the time money circulates broadly. Bitcoin eliminates this effect through fixed issuance and decentralized distribution.

Capital: Financial or economic resources, such as money or other assets, used to invest, generate income, or increase wealth. Bitcoin represents pristine capital, functioning as a secure and incorruptible store of economic energy.

Censorship Resistance: The property of a system or currency that prevents any authority, individual, or institution from censoring transactions. Bitcoin's decentralized structure ensures no single entity can block, reverse, or otherwise interfere with transactions.

Central Bank: A national authority responsible for managing monetary policy, issuing currency, and controlling interest rates. Bitcoin's creation was a direct response to central bank policies and their role in driving inflation.

Centralized: Controlled by a single authority, entity, or group, often leading to potential points of failure, censorship, or manipulation. Bitcoin explicitly opposes centralization, promoting distributed control to ensure network resilience.

Circulating Supply: The total amount of Bitcoin currently available and actively circulating within the market. It excludes permanently lost coins and coins not yet mined or released.

Code: Computer instructions or programming language written by developers, which forms the foundational software protocols governing Bitcoin's operation and security.

Coinbase: A major cryptocurrency exchange and brokerage platform headquartered in the United States, allowing users to buy, sell, and hold Bitcoin and other cryptocurrencies.

Coinbase Transaction: A special transaction included by miners as the first transaction in each new block, allowing them to collect the block reward and any associated transaction fees. Newly created bitcoin enter circulation through Coinbase transactions.

Cold Wallet/Cold Storage: A method of securely storing Bitcoin private keys offline, away from internet-connected devices, to protect against hacking, theft, and unauthorized access. Examples include hardware wallets, paper wallets, and air-gapped (physically isolated from unsecure networks) computers.

Collateral: An asset pledged as security to secure a loan, ensuring repayment. Bitcoin is increasingly used as collateral due to its liquidity, transparency, and reliable scarcity, transforming traditional lending practices.

Confirmation: A validation that occurs when a Bitcoin transaction is included in a block, securing it permanently on the blockchain. Multiple confirmations increase transaction security by making reversals increasingly difficult and costly.

Consensus: Agreement achieved across decentralized networks, ensuring all participants validate transactions and uphold identical ledger records. Bitcoin achieves consensus through Proof of Work, ensuring network reliability and immutability.

Consolidation: A phase in markets when prices stabilize within a defined range following volatility, usually preceding major price moves. Bitcoin's consolidation phases represent opportunities for strategic accumulation and reflect underlying market strength or indecision.

Consumer Price Index (CPI): A measure calculated by governments to track changes in the price of a basket of goods and services, used as an indicator of inflation. Bitcoin is considered a hedge against CPI inflation due to its fixed supply.

Crypto: A shorthand term for cryptocurrencies or related cryptographic technology, often casually used to refer broadly to digital assets, but specifically referring to the encryption technology that secures these digital assets.

Cryptocurrency: A digital asset or currency secured by cryptography, typically issued by a central entity or through an Initial Coin Offering (ICO). Cryptocurrencies usually depend on centralized decision-making, development teams, and governance models. Bitcoin is frequently grouped into this category because it is digital, cryptographically secured, and can function as a currency. However, Bitcoin fundamentally differs from cryptocurrencies because it has no issuer, no centralized governance, no ICO, and operates purely as decentralized, digital sound money. Bitcoin stands alone as a distinct innovation, separate from all other cryptocurrencies.

Cryptography: The science and practice of securing communication through encryption, ensuring security, privacy, and authenticity. Bitcoin leverages cryptographic algorithms to protect transaction integrity, secure private keys, maintain transparency, and prevent fraud.

Currency: A system or medium of exchange widely accepted as payment for goods and services. Bitcoin serves simultaneously as a currency, store of value, and unit of account, transcending traditional currency definitions.

Custodial/Custodian: A service or institution responsible for securely holding assets on behalf of users. Custodial Bitcoin services manage private keys and storage, introducing certain counterparty risks.

Cypherpunk: An activist who advocates strong cryptography, privacy, and decentralized technology to enhance individual freedom and resist government or corporate control. Bitcoin emerged directly from the cypherpunk movement, embracing its ideals and innovations.

Decentralization: The distribution of authority, control, or decision-making across a dispersed network without central governing bodies. Bitcoin's decentralization ensures censorship resistance, resilience, and network integrity.

Decentralized: Not controlled by any single entity, individual, or organization, ensuring independence from centralized authority. Bitcoin exemplifies decentralized finance, offering true economic sovereignty and autonomy.

Decentralized Finance (DeFi): Financial services built upon blockchain technology, enabling transactions, lending, borrowing, and trading without traditional intermediaries. Bitcoin serves as the foundational collateral within many DeFi protocols.

Difficulty: A measure of the complexity required for miners to solve the cryptographic puzzles needed to mine a new Bitcoin block. Difficulty adjusts automatically, maintaining consistent ten-minute block intervals despite changing network hash power.

Difficulty Adjustment: Bitcoin's mechanism for automatically recalibrating mining difficulty approximately every two weeks (every 2,016 blocks), ensuring stable block creation intervals and predictable Bitcoin issuance schedules.

Digital: Existing purely in electronic or virtual form, without physical presence. Bitcoin is entirely digital, enabling instant global transfer, perfect divisibility, and secure storage beyond physical constraints.

Digital Gold: A term frequently used to describe Bitcoin, emphasizing its properties as a scarce, portable, durable, and divisible store of value, offering advantages over traditional gold.

Digital Signature: A cryptographic method allowing for the secure, verifiable authentication of digital information. Bitcoin transactions utilize digital signatures to prove ownership and authenticity without revealing private keys.

Distributed Ledger: A decentralized database spread across multiple locations, participants, or nodes, ensuring transparency, resilience, and immutability. Bitcoin's blockchain is a distributed ledger publicly recording every transaction.

Double-Spending: A problem unique to digital currencies, referring to spending the same unit of currency multiple times. Bitcoin solved this previously unsolvable problem through its decentralized consensus and Proof of Work system.

Economic Sovereignty: The power of individuals or entities to independently control their own economic destinies, free from external manipulation. Bitcoin restores economic sovereignty through decentralized control and financial autonomy.

Encryption: A method of encoding information into unreadable ciphertext, protecting data privacy and security. Bitcoin employs advanced encryption techniques to secure transactions, wallets, and network communication.

Entropy: A measure of randomness, disorder, or unpredictability within a system. Bitcoin's cryptographic security relies heavily on entropy, ensuring randomness and unpredictability in generating secure private keys.

Epoch: In Bitcoin, refers to a period of 210,000 blocks, approximately four years, marking the interval between each Bitcoin halving event. Each epoch reduces the issuance rate of new Bitcoin, ensuring a predictable and diminishing supply over time.

Ethereum: A decentralized blockchain platform created by Vitalik Buterin in 2015, known primarily for enabling smart contracts—self-executing agreements that automatically trigger actions when specific conditions are met. Ethereum has its own native cryptocurrency called Ether (ETH), which is used to pay transaction fees ("gas") and incentivize participants. Unlike Bitcoin, Ethereum's primary purpose is to facilitate decentralized applications (dApps) and programmable transactions, allowing developers to create financial services, games, and complex contracts on a decentralized network.

Exchange: A marketplace facilitating the buying, selling, and trading of Bitcoin and other cryptocurrencies. Exchanges provide liquidity, price discovery, and entry points for investors and traders.

Exchange-Traded Fund (ETF): A regulated financial product traded on traditional stock exchanges, allowing investors to gain exposure to Bitcoin's price movements without having direct custody of coins. Spot Bitcoin ETFs hold actual Bitcoin, while futures ETFs track Bitcoin contracts rather than holding Bitcoin directly.

Fiat: Government-issued currency not backed by physical commodities like gold or silver, deriving value from government decree and public trust. Bitcoin directly opposes fiat currencies by offering mathematically enforced scarcity and incorruptibility.

Fractional Reserve Banking: A banking system in which commercial banks are required to hold only a fraction of customer deposits as reserves, lending out the rest. This structure allows banks to expand the money supply through credit creation, but it also creates systemic risk: If too many depositors demand their money at once (a "bank run"), the bank may not have enough reserves to cover withdrawals.

Fungible: The property of a currency or asset where individual units are interchangeable and indistinguishable. Bitcoin is fungible, as every Bitcoin unit holds equal value, enhancing its usability as money.

Game Theory: A branch of economics studying strategic decision-making, incentives, and competitive interactions. Bitcoin's incentives and protocol design leverage game theory to ensure cooperation, security, and network sustainability.

Genesis Block: The very first Bitcoin block mined by Satoshi Nakamoto on January 3, 2009, marking the start of Bitcoin's blockchain. Embedded within it was a message referencing financial system failures, highlighting Bitcoin's philosophical origins.

Halving: An event occurring approximately every four years (every 210,000 blocks), when Bitcoin's block reward for miners is cut in half. Halvings enforce Bitcoin's scarcity, ensuring a predictable and decreasing supply schedule until the maximum of 21 million coins is reached.

Hash: A unique cryptographic fingerprint generated by passing data through a cryptographic algorithm. Bitcoin uses SHA-256 hashes to securely link each block, creating an immutable chain resistant to alteration.

Hash Rate: The total computational power utilized by miners to validate and secure Bitcoin transactions. A higher hash rate signifies greater network security, resistance to attacks, and overall network health.

Hashing: The computational process used by miners to solve cryptographic puzzles as Proof of Work, transforming transaction data into secure hashes. Hashing secures the Bitcoin blockchain, ensuring its integrity and immutability.

Hot Wallet: An internet-connected wallet used to store Bitcoin, allowing convenient access and transactions. While practical, hot wallets have increased risk from hacking or otherwise unauthorized access compared to cold storage solutions.

Hyperinflation: An extreme economic condition where fiat currency rapidly loses purchasing power due to unchecked money printing, typically resulting in economic collapse. Bitcoin acts as a safeguard against hyperinflation due to its mathematically enforced scarcity.

Immutable: A state of permanence and unchangeability. Bitcoin's blockchain is immutable, ensuring transactions, once recorded, cannot be altered, censored, or reversed. This protects against fraud or corruption.

Inflation: A reduction in the purchasing power of a currency caused by increased money supply, often leading to rising prices. Bitcoin is deflationary by design, offering protection against inflationary monetary policies.

Intrinsic Value: The inherent value of an asset based on tangible properties or practical uses, independent of external market factors. Examples typically include precious metals used in jewelry or industrial materials with practical applications. Bitcoin, in contrast, has no intrinsic value—it derives its value from its monetary properties such as decentralization, censorship resistance, absolute scarcity, and secure network consensus, rather than from any physical or tangible use case.

Laser Eyes: A meme popularized on Crypto Twitter (CT, now X) and adopted by Bitcoin supporters symbolizing focus, a bullish confidence in Bitcoin's long-term value, and a commitment to holding until certain price targets are reached.

Ledger: A record of financial transactions. Bitcoin uses a public, distributed ledger (built on a blockchain), where every transaction is transparently recorded and verifiable by anyone on the network.

Leverage: Borrowing capital to amplify potential returns (and risks) in trading or investing. Leverage is common in Bitcoin derivatives trading, but excessive leverage significantly increases risks and volatility.

Lightning Network: A second-layer solution built on top of Bitcoin's blockchain, enabling near-instant, low-cost transactions by conducting smaller transactions off-chain and settling the net result on-chain, significantly improving Bitcoin's scalability.

Liquidity: The ease with which an asset can be quickly bought or sold without significantly affecting its price. Bitcoin's high liquidity allows efficient, rapid conversion into fiat or other assets across global markets.

Medium of Exchange: A function of money allowing goods and services to be exchanged. Bitcoin functions effectively as a digital medium of exchange, facilitating global, borderless transactions without intermediaries.

Miner: An individual or entity using computational power to validate transactions, secure the blockchain, and earn block rewards through the Proof of Work process. Miners are essential for maintaining Bitcoin's decentralized security.

Mining: The competitive process where miners utilize computational power to solve cryptographic puzzles, validate transactions, and secure the Bitcoin network, earning new bitcoin and transaction fees as rewards.

Mining Difficulty: A measure automatically adjusted by the Bitcoin network approximately every two weeks (2,016 blocks) to maintain consistent block creation intervals. Higher difficulty corresponds to increased computational resources required by miners.

Mining Pool: A collective of miners combining computational power to improve the chances of successfully mining blocks, distributing earned rewards proportionally based on each participant's contributed hash power.

Mining Reward: Compensation given to miners for successfully mining a new block. It includes newly minted Bitcoin (block subsidy) and collected transaction fees, incentivizing miners to secure the network.

Mining Rig: A specialized hardware setup designed explicitly for mining cryptocurrencies like Bitcoin, consisting typically of ASIC miners optimized to perform hashing computations efficiently.

Monetary: Pertaining to money or currency. Bitcoin represents a new monetary paradigm, free from centralized control, inflation, or governmental manipulation.

Monetary Policy: Strategies and actions taken by central banks to manage currency supply, inflation, and economic stability. Bitcoin's monetary policy is mathematically fixed, transparent, and unalterable, free from human manipulation or interference.

Money: A commonly accepted medium for exchange, storage of value, and unit of account. Bitcoin's absolute scarcity, divisibility, durability, portability, and fungibility make it superior money compared to traditional fiat currencies or any other form of money that has ever existed.

Moving Average: A technical analysis indicator showing an asset's average price over a specified period, smoothing short-term fluctuations and highlighting long-term trends. Widely used in Bitcoin trading and investing to identify support, resistance, and market sentiment.

Network: A decentralized, distributed group of interconnected participants or nodes maintaining Bitcoin's blockchain, collectively validating transactions and enforcing consensus rules.

Network Fee: A transaction fee voluntarily included by users to incentivize miners to prioritize and confirm transactions quickly. Higher network fees increase transaction priority, important when the network is congested.

Node: An individual computer running Bitcoin software, independently validating transactions and maintaining a complete copy of the blockchain. Nodes secure Bitcoin's decentralization and integrity by enforcing consensus rules.

Nonce: An arbitrary number miners repeatedly adjust in hashing calculations to find a valid cryptographic solution meeting network difficulty criteria. Successfully finding a nonce enables a miner to mine a new block.

Open Interest: The total number of active derivative contracts (such as futures or options) outstanding in financial markets, used as an indicator of market sentiment, liquidity, and potential volatility in Bitcoin markets.

Open-Source: Software whose source code is publicly accessible, allowing anyone to review, audit, modify, or contribute to development. Bitcoin is entirely open-source, ensuring transparency, security, and ongoing improvement.

Orange Pill: A metaphorical reference popularized in Bitcoin culture, inspired by the movie *The Matrix*, describing the transformative awakening to Bitcoin's philosophical, economic, and financial ideology.

Over-the-Counter (OTC): Trading of Bitcoin or other assets directly between two parties without involving exchanges, typically used for large transactions, minimizing market impact, and ensuring privacy.

Peer-to-Peer: Direct interactions or exchanges between parties without intermediaries. Bitcoin enables peer-to-peer financial transactions globally without central authorities or institutions.

Permissionless: A system that allows anyone to participate freely without needing authorization from central authorities or intermediaries. Bitcoin is inherently permissionless, enabling open participation.

Private Key: A secret cryptographic key used to access and control Bitcoin holdings, authorize transactions, and prove ownership. Secure private key management is essential, as loss results in permanent Bitcoin inaccessibility.

Programmability: The capacity of digital assets or platforms to execute automated actions or smart contracts based on predefined conditions. Bitcoin supports programmability through scripting capabilities and layered solutions like the Lightning Network.

Proof of Work (PoW): Bitcoin's consensus mechanism requiring miners to expend computational energy solving cryptographic puzzles, securing the blockchain, preventing fraud, and introducing new coins into circulation.

Protocol: The fundamental rules, standards, and procedures governing Bitcoin's operation, including transaction validation, consensus building, monetary issuance, and network participation.

Pseudonymous: A condition in which actions or transactions are linked to impersonal identifiers (such as Bitcoin addresses) rather than directly to personal identities. Bitcoin transactions are pseudonymous, visible publicly without revealing individual identities.

Public Address: A hashed version of a public key, serving as a destination for receiving Bitcoin payments. Public addresses ensure transactional privacy and security while enabling transparent verification on the blockchain.

Public Key: A cryptographic address derived mathematically from a private key, enabling the secure receipt of Bitcoin transactions. Public keys can be openly shared to receive funds without compromising security.

Public Ledger: Bitcoin's blockchain, a transparent, publicly accessible, immutable record of all transactions, maintained by distributed nodes worldwide.

Quantum Computing: An advanced computing paradigm leveraging quantum mechanics to process information exponentially faster than classical computers. Potentially a future threat to cryptographic security.

Quick Response (QR) Code: A scannable, two-dimensional barcode storing information such as Bitcoin addresses, enabling quick, error-free, and convenient transactions across the network.

Real-World Asset (RWA): A physical, tangible assets such as real estate, commodities, or other traditional investments. Tokenization enables the integration of RWAs with blockchain systems, expanding Bitcoin's role as collateral and financial infrastructure.

Recession: A significant and prolonged decline in economic activity, usually defined by two consecutive quarters of negative GDP growth. Bitcoin's limited supply and decentralized nature offer protection against recessionary economic instability.

Relative Strength Index (RSI): A technical analysis indicator measuring the momentum of recent price changes to identify if an asset is overbought or oversold. Used frequently in Bitcoin market analysis to anticipate price reversals or continuations.

Renewable Energy: Energy generated from sources that naturally replenish, such as solar, wind, or hydroelectric power. Bitcoin mining increasingly integrates renewable energy sources, incentivizing clean energy production and grid stabilization.

Resistance (Line/Level): A price level where increased selling pressure typically halts upward price movement. Resistance levels help traders anticipate market reversals or breakouts, an important concept in Bitcoin technical analysis.

Return on Investment (ROI): A performance measure used to evaluate profitability, calculated by dividing net profit by the initial investment amount. Bitcoin's historically high ROI demonstrates its potential as a superior investment asset.

S&P 500: A major US stock market index tracking the performance of 500 large-cap companies, used as a benchmark for economic health and traditional investment returns. Investors often compare Bitcoin's performance against the S&P 500 to evaluate its relative strength and potential as an asset.

Satoshi Nakamoto: The pseudonym of Bitcoin's creator, who introduced the Bitcoin white paper in 2008 and mined the first block (genesis block) in 2009. Satoshi's true identity remains unknown.

Satoshis (Sats): The smallest divisible unit of Bitcoin, named after its creator, Satoshi Nakamoto. One Bitcoin equals 100,000,000 satoshis (sats), useful for everyday microtransactions.

Scale: The capacity of a system to handle increased use or demand efficiently. Bitcoin scales through layered solutions such as the Lightning Network, enabling widespread global adoption without compromising decentralization or security.

Scale Invariance: A property of systems whose fundamental rules, mechanisms, or properties remain consistent and unchanged regardless of their size or usage. Bitcoin demonstrates scale invariance, as its monetary policy, security model, and fundamental rules remain the same whether it's used by thousands or billions of people.

Scarcity: The limited availability of a resource, which enhances its value. Bitcoin's absolute scarcity, capped mathematically at 21 million coins, provides it with enduring value preservation and economic superiority.

Secure Element: A specialized hardware component within hardware wallets or security devices protecting Bitcoin private keys from unauthorized access or extraction, ensuring enhanced security.

Securities and Exchange Commission (SEC): A US federal regulatory body overseeing securities markets, enforcing laws against market manipulation and fraud, and ensuring investor protection. SEC decisions regarding Bitcoin ETFs significantly influence institutional adoption and mainstream acceptance.

Seed Phrase/Recovery Seed: A sequence of twelve to twenty-four words generated during Bitcoin wallet creation, used to recover or restore wallet access if lost or compromised. Securely storing seed phrases is essential for long-term Bitcoin custody.

Self-Custody: The practice of securely holding one's Bitcoin private keys independently, without relying on third-party custodians. Self-custody ensures true financial sovereignty, eliminating counterparty risks.

Settlement: The finalization and fulfillment of financial transactions, ensuring irreversible transfer of ownership. Bitcoin's blockchain provides global, immutable, and rapid settlement, eliminating intermediary risks and delays.

SHA-256: The cryptographic hash function currently used by Bitcoin producing unique 256-bit hashes for securing transactions, mining operations, and maintaining blockchain integrity.

Short: A trading strategy involving selling borrowed assets in anticipation of price declines, intending to repurchase them at lower prices. Short selling Bitcoin carries significant risk due to its long-term appreciation trends.

Short Squeeze: A rapid price increase occurring when short sellers are forced to buy back positions due to rising prices, causing further upward pressure. Bitcoin markets frequently experience short squeezes, contributing to sharp price rallies.

Smart Contract: Self-executing contracts programmed to automatically enforce terms when specific conditions are met. Although Bitcoin's native scripting supports basic smart contracts, more complex smart contract functionality is provided through layers like Rootstock.

Smart Token: A digital token programmed to execute specific actions automatically under predetermined conditions, enhancing functionality and versatility within blockchain ecosystems.

Sound Money: Money that retains value over time, free from manipulation or excessive inflation. Bitcoin embodies sound money principles through mathematically guaranteed scarcity and decentralized control.

Stablecoins: Cryptocurrencies pegged to stable assets, typically fiat currencies like the US dollar, maintaining price stability. Often used as a hedge against volatility, stablecoins facilitate seamless trading and global financial inclusion alongside Bitcoin.

Stocktwits: A social media platform focused on finance and investing, where traders and investors share real-time ideas, charts, and commentary. Similar to Twitter/X in format, but centered specifically on stocks, cryptocurrencies, and markets, Stocktwits is often used to gauge market sentiment.

Store of Value: An asset's ability to maintain or increase its perceived value over time. Bitcoin's immutability, decentralized security, and absolute scarcity make it a premier global store of value.

Supercomputer: A highly advanced computer capable of performing extremely fast calculations. Bitcoin's global mining network, powered collectively by millions of specialized mining rigs, effectively operates as a decentralized supercomputer, securing transactions and consensus.

Supply and Demand: Economic forces determining price based on the relationship between available supply and consumer demand. Bitcoin's fixed supply and rising global demand significantly influence its long-term price appreciation.

Support Level: A price level at which buying pressure prevents further downward price movement. Traders monitor support levels to identify potential buying opportunities or market reversals.

Swing Trading: A trading strategy aimed at capturing short- to medium-term price movements, often holding positions from days to weeks. Bitcoin's volatility and clear technical patterns make it attractive for swing trading strategies.

Technical Analysis: A method of evaluating investments by analyzing statistical trends from historical price movements and volume. Widely utilized in Bitcoin markets, technical analysis helps traders identify patterns, trends, support, and resistance levels.

Technical Indicators: Statistical tools that derive information from price, volume, or open interest data, assisting traders in identifying trends, reversals, or market momentum. Common indicators in Bitcoin markets include RSI, moving averages, and Bollinger Bands.

Ticker: An abbreviation or symbol representing an asset on trading platforms or exchanges. Bitcoin's globally recognized ticker symbol is "BTC."

Timechain: The original term used by Satoshi Nakamoto to describe Bitcoin's blockchain, emphasizing the importance of cryptographically secured, chronological sequencing of blocks and transactions. It represents Bitcoin's immutable proof-of-time mechanism.

Timestamp: A digital record indicating the precise date and time a transaction or block is created or confirmed. Bitcoin uses timestamps to verify transaction orders, preventing double-spending and ensuring blockchain integrity.

Token: A digital representation of value or asset on a blockchain, distinct from the native cryptocurrency itself. Tokens may represent assets, utilities, rights, or other forms of value within blockchain ecosystems.

Tokenization: The process of representing real-world assets digitally on a blockchain, enhancing liquidity, transparency, and accessibility. Bitcoin-based solutions and sidechains facilitate the tokenization of diverse assets, from real estate to securities.

Trading Volume: The total number of Bitcoin units traded within a given period. High trading volume indicates robust market activity, liquidity, and helps traders gauge market sentiment and potential volatility.

TradingView: A widely used online platform providing advanced charting tools, real-time market data, and social networking features. Popular among Bitcoin traders for performing technical analysis and sharing insights.

Transaction: An entry or exchange recorded on the Bitcoin blockchain, transferring Bitcoin from one wallet address to another. Transactions are validated by miners and permanently secured onto the blockchain.

Transaction Fee: A small fee paid by users to miners for confirming and validating their transactions on the Bitcoin network. The amount of this fee influences the priority and speed of transaction confirmation. During periods of network congestion, higher transaction fees are required to ensure prompt processing and inclusion in the blockchain.

Trust: Confidence in the reliability, integrity, and ability of entities or systems. Bitcoin reduces the necessity of trust in institutions by replacing it with mathematical proof, transparency, and decentralized consensus.

Trustless: A quality of systems operating without requiring trust in third parties or centralized entities. Bitcoin achieves trustlessness through decentralized validation, cryptography, and consensus, ensuring reliability without human intermediaries.

Unbanked: Individuals without access to traditional financial services or banking infrastructure. Bitcoin offers unprecedented financial inclusion for unbanked populations by providing accessible, global, and permissionless financial services.

Unconfirmed: A Bitcoin transaction broadcast to the network but not yet included in a mined block. Transactions remain unconfirmed until validated and secured by miners, affecting transaction finality and security.

Unit of Account: A standard numerical unit of measurement used to price goods, services, and debts. Bitcoin increasingly functions as a global unit of account, providing consistent pricing stability and international transactional convenience.

Unregulated: Systems or markets operating without government or institutional oversight or control. Bitcoin's decentralized nature means it operates largely outside traditional regulatory frameworks, though exchanges and custodians often face local regulatory requirements.

Unspent Transaction Output (UTXO): Bitcoin's fundamental accounting method tracking coin ownership through transaction outputs rather than account balances. UTXOs function similarly to physical cash, enhancing transaction transparency and security.

Utility Mining: Mining practices designed to utilize excess or otherwise wasted energy sources, such as stranded natural gas, methane flares, or surplus renewable energy, converting environmental liabilities into economic value through Bitcoin mining.

Virus: Metaphorically used in Bitcoin culture, describing how awareness, adoption, and understanding of Bitcoin spread organically and uncontrollably, akin to viral phenomena, rapidly shifting global financial perspectives, e.g., "The Bitcoin Virus."

Volatility: The degree to which the price of an asset fluctuates within a short time. Bitcoin is known for its volatility, reflecting rapid adoption cycles, evolving market maturity, and shifting global sentiment.

Volume: The total quantity of Bitcoin traded within a defined period, indicating market liquidity, activity, and trader participation. Volume analysis assists traders in assessing market strength, validating price movements, and anticipating future trends.

Wallet: A digital interface or tool used to store, manage, send, and receive Bitcoin, secured by cryptographic keys. Wallets can be software-based (hot wallets), hardware devices, or offline storage solutions (cold wallets).

Wallet Address: An alphanumeric identifier generated from public keys, used to receive Bitcoin transactions securely and privately. Wallet addresses enhance transaction security and privacy, allowing users to manage funds independently.

Weak Hands: Market participants who easily panic or sell their Bitcoin positions quickly during price declines, often driven by emotional responses or lack of conviction. Contrasted by "strong hands," who hold Bitcoin through market volatility.

Wrapped Bitcoin (WBTC): An Ethereum-based token pegged one-to-one with Bitcoin, allowing Bitcoin to participate in Ethereum-based decentralized finance (DeFi) services and liquidity pools. However, WBTC introduces counterparty risk that is not present in the native Bitcoin ecosystem.

Wyckoff Method: A trading framework developed by Richard Wyckoff that analyzes how large market participants accumulate and distribute assets. It breaks market cycles into phases—accumulation, reaccumulation, distribution, and redistribution—to help traders interpret price structure and volume. Though originally applied to stocks, many Bitcoin traders find Wyckoff patterns useful for identifying long-term market behavior.

Acknowledgments

Everything we know about Bitcoin we learn from those who have walked the path before us. They explored, explained, and shared their knowledge, making this complex technology accessible. The learning journey is universal, but our personal awakening—the moment the switch flips—is unique for each of us. Mine was mental, emotional, spiritual, and even physical. I owe a deep debt of gratitude to the following people for enlightening and supporting me throughout my journey.

I begin by thanking my wife, Nicole, who bore the brunt of my Bitcoin awakening, especially when I couldn't stop talking about it. Your patience, support, and encouragement have meant everything. I love you.

I thank my parents, Al and Barbara Marulli. You offered your love and excitement even though Bitcoin is not part of your reality.

Special thanks to Wicked (@w_s_bitcoin) for allowing me to feature his Bitcoin Block Subsidy Table. His graphics and work continue to inspire and educate the Bitcoin community.

Thanks to my real estate colleague and friend Heath Honbarrier for reading an early draft of the manuscript. Your understanding of the content inspired me to continue.

Thanks to my trading friend Bob Prestyly for convincing me to join Crypto Twitter and for the many conversations over the last eighteen months.

Thanks to my friend and real estate colleague Nick Nickerson for listening, and to my colleague and friend Carol Bernton for your kindness and support.

Thanks to my dear friend George Fiedler for embracing my ideas and nudging me to move forward.

Thanks to my friend Daniel Fort. The telepathic UTXOs between us are everlasting.

Thanks to my lifelong friends Gino Cicerchia and Adam Wilson for being there when I needed you.

Thanks to Matthew Jordan Storm and Leah Martin. You've always been there for me.

To the team that helped make this a reality: My Word Publishing; Amanda Miller, an incredible publishing manager; Cheryl Jaclin Isaac of Cheryl JI Editing, whose insight, precision, and encouragement elevated this book beyond what I thought possible; James Hallman, editor with WriteWorks, whose editorial work helped transition the manuscript from draft to professional form; Aga Siuda and Aline Regis of Graphroots Design, who built my website and designed the book cover; Matt Draper for superb photography; The Law Offices of Patricia Jo Stone; Khalid Rasheed for the illustrations; and Dani Greer for getting me started on the editing process.

I am incredibly thankful to all of you who shared your knowledge and paved the way for my understanding. It is impossible to thank everyone who influenced and inspired me, but special thanks to: Satoshi Nakamoto, Andreas Antonopoulos, Samson Mow, Michael Saylor, Tim Kotzman, Saifedean Ammous, Hal Finney, Knut Svanholm, BTC Sessions, The Space–Denver, Terence Michael, Lyn Alden, Jack Mallers, Nick Szabo, Adam Back, Preston J. Byrne, JAN3, Bevan Waite, Jeff Booth, Robert Breedlove, Grant Cardone, Gary Cardone, Isabel Foxen Duke, Tad Smith, Natalie Brunell, Uncle Rockstar Developer, Max Keiser, Stacy Herbert, Leon Wankum, Natalie Smolenski, Pierre Rochard, Matthew Kratter, Jason P. Lowery, Ray Dalio, Steve Nison, Crypto

Twitter, Mechanic @GrassFedBitcoin, @hodlorado, @Bitcoin_Teddy, @sminston_with, @bitcoin__apex, @TechDev_52, @apsk32, and @Giovann35084111. Without your dedication and generosity, none of this would have been possible.

And finally, to my family and friends who supported me along the way, thank you all. Your contributions, patience, and guidance made this book a reality.

NOTES

INTRODUCTION

1. Michelle Conlin, "Big US banks withstand Fed's commercial real estate shock scenario," Reuters, June 26, 2024, https://www.reuters.com/markets/us/big-us-banks-withstand-feds-commercial-real-estate-shock-scenario-2024-06-26.

1. INCEPTION

1. Satoshi Nakamoto, "Bitcoin: A Peer-to-Peer Electronic Cash System," October 31, 2008, https://bitcoin.org/bitcoin.pdf.
2. James Royal, "Bitcoin's price history and historical data (2009–2025)," Bankrate, August 5, 2025, https://www.bankrate.com/investing/bitcoin-price-history/.
3. The term "fiat" originates from Latin, meaning "let it be done" or "it shall be," referring to currencies issued by government decree with no intrinsic value or physical backing, such as gold or silver. The US dollar became a fiat currency in 1971 when Nixon took us off the gold standard.
4. To differentiate, Bitcoin is capitalized when referring to the network itself and is lowercase when referring to the digital asset.

2. WHO IS SATOSHI NAKAMOTO?

1. Aniket Verma, "Bitcoin Creator Satoshi Nakamoto Once Said He Had No Time To 'Convince' Non-Believers: Why Coinbase CEO Brought It Up After 15 Years," Benzinga, July 30, 2025, https://www.benzinga.com/crypto/cryptocurrency/25/07/46713430/bitcoin-creator-satoshi-nakamoto-once-said-he-had-no-time-to-convince-non-believers-why-coinbase-ceo-brought-it-up-after-15-years.

3. THE GENESIS BLOCK

1. "Chancellor on Brink of Second Bailout for Banks," *The Times*, January 3, 2009, https://www.thetimes03jan2009.com.

4. THE HALVING

1. Vineet Nair, "How Many Bitcoin Are Lost?" Ledger Academy, May 7, 2025,

https://www.ledger.com/academy/topics/economics-and-regulation/how-many-bitcoin-are-lost-ledger.

2. Andrew Kamsky, How Much Bitcoin Will Remain by 2028? A Deep Dive Into Having, Scarcity & Supply," CCN, April 28, 2025, https://www.ccn.com/education/crypto/how-much-bitcoin-will-remain-by-2028-supply-and-scarcity/#:~:text=New%20research%20from%20Bitwise%20Asset,%2C%20and%20governments%20(1.4%25).

3. In this book, "inflation" refers to monetary inflation (growth of the money supply), unless otherwise noted.

7. The System – Proof of Work, Miners, and Hash Rate

1. EPA, "Understanding Global Warming Potentials," accessed August 20, 2025, https://www.epa.gov/ghgemissions/understanding-global-warming-potentials; ipcc, *AR6 Synthesis Report*, accessed August 20, 2025, https://www.ipcc.ch/report/ar6/syr/.

2. "HIVE Digital Signs Agreement to Develop 100 MW Hydroelectric Data Center in Paraguay, Targeting to Reach 12 Exahash Next Year," Newsfile, July 31, 2024, https://www.newsfilecorp.com/release/218447.

10. The Importance of Self-Custody

1. The expression was popularized by Andreas Antonopoulos, one of Bitcoin's most influential educators and a figure I hold in the highest regard. His work is essential for anyone serious about understanding Bitcoin.

2. Bradley Peak, "The Mt Gox Bitcoin heist, and why is still matters," Cointelegraph, updated July 9, 2025, https://cointelegraph.com/learn/articles/the-mt-gox-bitcoin-heist; Tim Copeland, "The complex story of the QuadrigaCX $190 million scandal," Decrypt, March 13, 2019, https://decrypt.co/5853/complete-story-quadrigacx-190-million; U.S. Securities and Exchange Commission, "Genesis Agrees to Pay $21 Million Penalty to Settle SEC Charges, Press Releases, March 19, 2024, https://www.sec.gov/newsroom/press-releases/2024-37#:~:text=Genesis%20and%20two%20affiliates%20filed,or%20Updated:%20March%2019%2C%202024; Nathan Reiff, "The Collapse of FTX: What Went Wrong With the Crypto Exchange," Investopedia, October 10, 2024, https://www.investopedia.com/what-went-wrong-with-ftx-6828447.

3. Michael Saylor, "Bitcoin is money that they can't take away," YouTube video, Swan Bitcoin, February 24, 2025, https://www.youtube.com/shorts/hWiBumS3qV0.

4. Danielle du Toit, "Stefan Thomas: The Man Behind Bitcoin's Lost Millions," *Coinpaper*, January 14, 2025, https://coinpaper.com/6899/stefan-thomas-the-man-behind-bitcoin-s-lost-millions.

5. Issy Ronald, "Man who lost $800 million bitcoin in landfill wants to buy the

garbage dump," CNN World, updated February 14, 2025, https://www.cnn.com/2025/02/14/uk/james-howells-landfill-bitcoin-gbr-intl-scli.

13. Analyzing Bitcoin Markets

1. "Bitcoin At Risk of Supply Shock As ETF Issues Buy More BTC Than Was Produced in December," TradingView, January 7, 2025, https://www.tradingview.com/news/newsbtc:47a259ba7094b:0-bitcoin-at-risk-of-supply-shock-as-etf-issues-buy-more-btc-than-was-produced-in-december.
2. Rubén Villahermosa Chaves, *The Wyckoff Methodology in Depth* (self-published, 2018).

15. Inflation & Entropy – The Struggle Against Disorder

1. Brian Baker, "Money market yields are high – Why that may not last and where to invest instead," Bankrate, July 30, 2024, https://www.bankrate.com/investing/money-market-fund-rates/#:~:text=As%20the%20Fed%20begins%20to,be%20reinvesting%20at%20lower%20rates.
2. "Nixon and the End of the Bretton Woods System, 1973–1973," Office of the Historian, accessed August 19, 2025, https://history.state.gov/milestones/1969-1976/nixon-shock; "Billions of Dollars, Seasonally Adjusted, Monthly," FRED, updated July 22, 2025, https://fred.stlouisfed.org/series/M2SL#; "Table 24. Historical Consumer Price Index for All Urban Consumers (CPI-U): U.S. city average," BLS, accessed August 19, 2025, https://www.bls.gov/cpi/tables/historical-cpi-u-201710.pdf.
3. "Broad money growth (annual %)," World Bank Group, International Financial Statistics Database, International Monetary Fund (IMF), accessed August 19, 2025, https://data.worldbank.org/indicator/FM.LBL.BMNY.ZG.
4. Fid Backhouse et al., "Hyperinflation in the Weimar Republic," Britannica, German History, accessed August 6, 2025, https://www.britannica.com/technology/printing-press.
5. Steve H. Hanke, "Zimbabwe's Hyperinflation: The Correct Number is 89 Sextillion Percent," CATO Institute, June 3, 2016, https://www.cato.org/blog/zimbabwes-hyperinflation-correct-number-89-sextillion-percent.
6. Frank Muci, "Why did Venezuela's economy collapse?" Economics Observatory, September 23, 2024, https://www.economicsobservatory.com/why-did-venezuelas-economy-collapse.

16. The Shifting Role of Real Estate

1. Preston Pysh, host, *Bitcoin Fundamentals*, *We Study Billionaires*, podcast, "Bitcoin & Real Estate w/ Leon Wankum," The Investor's Podcast Network,

January 9, 2023, https://www.theinvestorspodcast.com/bitcoin-fundamentals/bitcoin-real-estate-leon-wankum.

2. Caitlin Cahalan, "Warren Buffett's Berkshire Hathaway predicts major housing market shift soon," TheStreet, July 20, 2025, https://www.thestreet.com/real-estate/warren-buffetts-berkshire-hathaway-predicts-major-housing-market-shift-soon.

3. Richard C. K. Burdekin, "The US Money Explosion of 2020, Monetarism and Inflation: Plagued by History?" *Scientific Research* 11, no. 11 (2020), https://www.scirp.org/journal/paperinformation?paperid=104299.

4. William Diamond et al., "Printing Away the Mortgages: Fiscal Inflation and the Post-Covid Housing Boom," Cowles Foundation for Research in Economics, March 22, 2023, https://cowles.yale.edu/sites/default/files/2023-04/fiscal_housing_covid_v20230320.pdf.

5. Frank Corva, "Newmarket Capital Launches Battery Finance, Bitcoin-Collateralized Loan Strategy," *Bitcoin Magazine*, November 25, 2024, https://bitcoinmagazine.com/business/newmarket-capital-launches-battery-finance-bitcoin-collateralized-loan-strategy.

6. Oscar Nunez, "First Direct Wallet-To-Wallet Cryptocurrency Real Estate Sale Completed At The Rider Residences In Miami," Florida Yimby, April 27, 2025, https://floridayimby.com/2025/04/first-direct-wallet-to-wallet-cryptocurrency-real-estate-sale-completed-at-the-rider-residences-in-miami.html.

7. David Marulli, "The Day Bitcoin Ate Real Estate," Proof of Work Press, April 28, 2025, https://davidmarulli.substack.com/p/the-day-bitcoin-ate-real-estate.

17. Egalitarianism

1. Isabel Foxen Duke, host, *Bitcoin Rails*, podcast, "How To Build a Bitcoin Career," Best In Slot, February 3, 2025, https://open.spotify.com/episode/6cpEbp6UGZuac3eleR4c3R.

20. Banks and Unbanking

1. "Bitcoin: another record low for reserves on exchanges," The Cryptonomist, July 8, 2025, https://en.cryptonomist.ch/2025/07/08/bitcoin-another-record-low-for-reserves-on-exchanges/; Nancy Lubale, "Less than 15% Bitcoin left on crypto exchanges signals 'supply problem,'" Cointelegraph, July 1, 2025, https://cointelegraph.com/news/less-than-15-bitcoin-left-on-crypto-exchanges-signals-supply-problem?utm_source=chatgpt.com.

22. Michael Saylor's Epiphany

1. Daniel Prince, host, *Once BITten*, podcast, Michael Saylor and Daniel Prince, November 13, 2020, https://www.youtube.com/watch?v=WSKOueBeOns&list=PLy1T4fro4NP-bMdgaYrYMI35855Qj-EUd&index=1.

2. Kevin Stankiewicz, "MicroStrategy CEO defends debt-financed bitcoin buys, compares it to investing early in Facebook," CNBC, Cryptocurrency, July 30, 2021, https://www.cnbc.com/2021/07/30/microstrategy-ceo-defends-bitcoin-buys-compares-it-to-investing-early-in-facebook.html.

3. "MicroStrategy Announces Second Quarter 2020 Financial Results," Business Wire, July 28, 2020, https://www.businesswire.com/news/home/20200728005846/en/MicroStrategy-Announces-Second-Quarter-2020-Finan cial-Results.

4. Michael Saylor (@saylor), "Bitcoin is money. Everything else is credit." X, July 2, 2025, https://x.com/saylor/status/1940405588548345887?lang=en.

5. "Purchases," Strategy, last updated August 19, 2025, https://www.strategy.com/purchases.

6. Bitcoin News (@BitcoinNewsCom), "I'll be buying at the top forever," X, March 5, 2024, https://x.com/BitcoinNewsCom/status/1765210919942889520.

7. Edan Yago, "Bitcoin Treasury Companies Are the New Altcoins," *Forbes*, Digital Assets, updated July 31, 2025, https://www.forbes.com/sites/edanyago/2025/07/31/bitcoin-treasury-companies-are-the-new-altcoins/.

8. Strategy, "MicroStrategy Announces Pricing of Offering of Convertible Senior Notes," December 9, 2020, https://www.strategy.com/press/microstrategy-announces-pricing-of-offering-of-convertible-senior-notes_12-09-2020?utm; Strategy, "MicroStrategy to Redeem $1.05B of 2027 Convertible Notes and Settle All Conversion Requests in Shares," January 24, 2025, https://www.strate gysoftware.com/pt/press/microstrategy-to-redeem-1b-of-2027-convertible-notes-settle-all-conversion-requests-in-shares_01-24-2025?utm; U.S. Securities and Exchange Commission, "MicroStrategy Incorporated," Form 10-Q, May 1, 2024, https://www.sec.gov/Archives/edgar/data/1050446/000095017024051230/mstr-20240331.htm?utm; Strategy, "Strategy Completes $2 Billion Offering of 0% Convertible Senior Notes Due 2030," February 24, 2025, https://www.strategy.com/press/strategy-completes-2-billion-offering-of-convertible-senior-notes-due-2030_02-24-2025?utm.

9. U.S. Securities and Exchange Commission, "MicroStrategy Up to $21,000,000,000 Class A Common Stock," October 30, 2024, https://www.sec.gov/Archives/edgar/data/1050446/000119312524247536/d905160d424b5.htm?utm; U.S. Securities and Exchange Commission, "MicroStrategy Up to $750,000,000 Class A Common Stock," August 1, 2023, https://www.sec.gov/Archives/edgar/data/1050446/000119312523200621/d533407d424b5.htm?utm.

10. Strategy, "Strategy Announces Second Quarter 2025 Financial Results," July 31, 2025, https://www.strategy.com/press/strategy-announces-second-quarter-2025-financial-results_07-31-2025?utm; Strategy, "MicroStrategy Announces Pricing of Strike Preferred Stock Offering (STRK), January 31, 2025; https://www.strategy.com/press/microstrategy-announces-pricing-of-strike-preferred-stock-offering-strk_01-31-2025; Strategy, "Strategy Announces Pricing of STRF Perpetual Preferred Stock," March 21, 2025, https://www.strategy.com/press/strategy-announces-pricing-of-strf-perpetual-preferred-stock_03-21-2025; Strategy, "Strategy Announces Pricing of Initial Public Offering of STRD Stock," June 6, 2025, https://www.strategy.com/press/strategy-announces-pric

ing-of-initial-public-offering-of-strd-stock_06-08-2025?utm; Strategy, "Strategy Announces Pricing of STRC Perpetual Preferred Stock," July 25, 2025, https://www.strategy.com/press/strategy-announces-pricing-of-strc-perpetual-preferred-stock_07-25-2025?utm.

11. Pedro Solimano, "Microstrategy Has Outperformed All S&P 500 Companies Thanks to Bitcoin," The Defiant, September 23, 2024, https://thedefiant.io/news/markets/microstrategy-has-outperformed-all-s-and-p-500-companies-thanks-to-bitcoin.

12. "Bitcoin News Today: MicroStrategy's Saylor Signals Possible New Bitcoin Purchase," AInvest, Coin World, August 17, 2025, https://www.ainvest.com/news/bitcoin-news-today-microstrategy-saylor-signals-bitcoin-purchase-2508/.

13. Bitcoin Advisory, "Bitcoin is an enlightened and peaceful way … demonetizes the incentives for war," Instagram video reel, accessed August 6, 2025.

24. Global Impact

1. "Fiat Currency Graveyard: A History of Monetary Folly," Gini Foundation, accessed August 6, 2025, https://ginifoundation.org/kb/fiat-currency-graveyard-a-history-of-monetary-folly.

2. Adam Bisno, "How Hyperinflation Heralded the Fall of German Democracy," *Smithsonian Magazine*, May 23, 2023, https://www.smithsonianmag.com/history/how-hyperinflation-heralded-the-fall-of-german-democracy-180982204/; C. Jennings, "Hungary's 1946 Hyperinflation: The Worst Inflation in History and the Fall of the Pengő," Planet Banknote, May 28, 2025, https://planetbanknote.com/banknote-blog/hungarys-1946-hyperinflation-the-worst-inflation-in-history-and-the-fall-of-the-peng/?srsltid=AfmBOor2baYia ful7H6TXYRZ9054Uw59egpYAExemO4_KvSFakfsGD6b; Tejvan Pettinger, "Hyper Inflation in Zimbabwe," Economics Help.org, November 13, 2019, https://www.economicshelp.org/blog/390/inflation/hyper-inflation-in-zimbabwe/; Corina Pons, "Venezuela 2016 inflation hits 800 percent, GDP shrinks 19 percent," Reuters, January 20, 2017, https://www.reuters.com/article/business/venezuela-2016-inflation-hits-800-percent-gdp-shrinks-19-percent-document-idUSKBN154243/.

25. Bitcoin, War, and the Battle for Hash Power

1. Jason Paul Lowery, *Softwar: A Novel Theory on Power Projection and the National Strategic Significance of Bitcoin* (independently published, 2023).

2. "Bitcoin mining electricity update: new data," University of Cambridge Judge Business School, May 17, 2022, https://www.jbs.cam.ac.uk/2022/bitcoin-mining-electricity-update-new-data/; *Cambridge Digital Mining Report, Global Operations, Sentiment, and Energy Use*, Cambridge Centre for Alternative Finance, University of Cambridge Judge Business School, April 2025, https://

www.jbs.cam.ac.uk/wp-content/uploads/2025/04/2025-04-cambridge-digital-mining-industry-report.pdf.

ABOUT THE AUTHOR

David Marulli is not your typical Bitcoin influencer. He isn't part of the trendy crypto crowd on social media, nor is he a recognizable personality frequently showcased on YouTube or podcasts. Instead, he brings a rare and valuable perspective rooted in three decades of experience in high-level commercial real estate transactions. Over his career, he has personally transacted more than $1 billion in commercial real estate deals, advising and collaborating with high-net-worth investors managing portfolios exceeding $100 million.

A deeply respected industry veteran since 1995, David witnessed firsthand how traditional real estate, despite its longstanding prominence as a store of wealth, had begun to lose ground to the revolutionary potential of Bitcoin. After discovering Bitcoin, he realized that traditional property investments could no longer fully leverage his expertise or provide the long-term financial freedom he sought. Compelled by what he learned, David evolved from a seasoned businessman into a dedicated Bitcoin maximalist.

Outside of his professional career, David has always identified as an artist at heart, passionately creating abstract expressionist paintings. His work was featured in Times Square in 2023. To bring his insights about Bitcoin to the world, he paused his artistic pursuits, channeling his creative energy instead into writing this book.

David invites readers to share in the transformative insights he's discovered on his journey from real estate expert to Bitcoin advocate. For more information, check out www.davidmarulli.com.